Teach Twice

Daniel García González

First edition
Bilbao, July 2020

All rights reserved

© Daniel García González
Ediciones Triple Eñe / TapaBlanda

ISBN: 978-84-122075-3-8

Last revised: 1st July 2020

Original title:
'*Enseña dos veces: Cómo configurar talleres con MOODLE
para que tus estudiantes se corrijan entre sí*'

to the non-conformist teacher

Dear reader:

This is the English version of my Spanish book 'Enseña dos veces'. It would have been impossible without the help of John (Glasgow) and William (Builth Wells) who helped me to correct many of my mistakes with Shakespeare's language.

Please, if you are confused by any of my expressions or find any other type of error, I would appreciate it if you could let me know, so that I can modify it and improve it in future revisions.

Thank you very much in advance

Daniel

About this book:

This book began life as a 'Peer-Assessment with Moodle Workshops' course, taught in the University of the Basque Country's teacher-training programme.

Since the initial course, other Further and Higher education institutions have adopted subsequent editions as a professional development tool. Aimed at university teaching staff, the course has been used widely to increase the quality of teaching and learning in these institutions.

Over the years, course participants have often shown an interest in having the course materials gathered into one volume, the result of which is contained in the present edition.

About the author:

Daniel García González has taught Journalism at the University of the Basque Country since 2001, covering writing, design, business, and computer graphics. His main research interest at present is the application of technology in journalism.

He holds degrees in Advertising & Public Relations and Journalism from the University of the Basque Country; and a degree in Law from the University of Deusto. He obtained his doctorate with a thesis on the use of computer graphics in the Spanish press. He has also worked as a graphic artist and visualisation designer at the El Correo newspaper in Bilbao, Spain.

He would be delighted to receive any comments, questions, doubts or suggestions.

DANIEL.GARCIA@EHU.EUS

Additional Content:

More information, forums, FAQs, sample Workshops etc. can be found at

WWW.TEACHTWICE.NET

The Settings

The Five Phases

Origins

The villain of the piece

Around the turn of the century I was a new teacher and still brimming with enthusiasm for teaching (yes, those halcyon days!). One day, two students from one of my afternoon groups accosted me in the corridor to ask me about something that was bothering them. They had heard whispers that the morning group were progressing more slowly than theirs, and had covered less course material. They were concerned that their exam would be more demanding than the morning group's. There's nothing new about students complaining, right? The thing is, one of the students, insisting that the exams be fair and balanced, said with a straight face that he had «***the right to know less***».

This expression certainly raised an eyebrow at the time. But the more I thought about it, the more I realised that it reveals a deeper, slightly unnerving, truth about our work. It's hard to imagine someone going to a concert, a cinema or a restaurant with a similar attitude: –«*Well pardon me! I am paying for this, but... I insist the band cuts their set short. I insist they don't show the whole film. I insist the portions should be small!*»–.

And yet that's the way it is in the classroom. When, for whatever reason, we cut a class short, the general response is one of delight. Likewise, when we utter the magic words – «*...well, we're almost out of time. Let's leave it there for today*»–: There has never been a known case, anywhere, of students forming an angry mob, demanding that the class be completed strictly as planned.

In the eyes of our students, we are examiner first and teacher second. We like to think of ourselves as collaborators, working and learning alongside our students, but in their eyes, we are judge and jury.

Professor Eric Mazur of Harvard University described summative assessment –the exam– as '***the silent killer of learning***'. For many years, I too have felt that the exam is the villain of the piece. Though we are supposed to be teachers, we are regularly required to dedicate more of our energy to 'the exam' (and the varying roles it forces us to play), than to developing great learning experiences.

Discovering computer-assisted peer-evaluation has restored my faith in education. Preparing good quality workshops brought the intellectual challenge back into my work. Nowadays, I feel that the design of each activity, and creating each rubric is worth spending time on. I see that it bears fruit. For that reason, I have tried to simplify the technical aspects so that they are not blockers for anyone who wants to jump right in. Likewise, I strongly believe that the goal is great peer-assessment, and not great technology. It should never become an obstacle.

In brief

What is a peer-assessment workshop?

In a paired activity assigned to students, rather than each student simply submitting the exercise, we also require them to assess submissions from other students. This can be in the form of a simple questionnaire, rubric, or some other framework provided by the teacher. Teachers have been doing this kind of thing in classrooms since the year dot, providing simple forms between pairs and calculating a mark by hand. Nothing new there.

Where does Moodle come in?

Moodle is a free, open-source software platform that allows us to manage this kind of assessment online. It handles the initial submission of assignments and the subsequent peer-assessments; in such a way that a student can peer-assess not only their partner's or group's work, but the work of as many students as is required. Moodle will also help distribute feedback to students and will perform the calculations required to grade the work. It will publish and share those too. The teacher could, of course, do this by hand, but at the cost of a lot of extra work and an obscene amount of time.

And what makes Moodle indispensable?

The system calculates an average mark for the piece of work itself, based on the score awarded to it by its assessors. However, in the background it also carries out the second part of the assessment. It calculates a second mark for each participant, based on how well they assess their colleagues. The system can even detect whether individuals are working in 'bad faith' or just plain not trying hard enough. As such, the student cohort starts to self-police. With the help of Moodle's statistics logic, students work together to produce grades akin to what the teacher would award. As such, the teacher is relieved of their traditional roles –formal-assessor, judge, jury– and instead simply supervises the assessment process and focusses on pedagogy. It takes **tens of thousands of calculations** to arrive at those grades, which would become overwhelming if we had to perform them manually. It is probably fair to say that this kind of peer-assessment is only really feasible if it supported by technology.

How this book explains it:

Each reader will have their own particular requirements. Some of you will have tried to set up Workshops previously and will be reading with specific questions in mind. Others will be totally new to it all. For that reason, this book starts from first principles. Someone who has never tried to set up a Workshop can follow step-by-step instructions to get started. For more experienced readers, this book serves as a reference skipped over with many useful tricks; the sections are ordered sequentially to make the right information easy to find.

There are two main barriers to using Workshop:

1. Moodle is the most widely-adopted Learning Management System (LMS) in the world, due to its versatility and speed. However, these advantages are counterbalanced by the greatest weakness of the platform: **its dull, text-based interface**, which leaves a lot to be desired in terms of user-friendliness. This can cause beginners to feel confused; not understanding what the various labels and tags mean, being unsure of the layout of the screens and menus and so on. For that reason, it's essential that users take time to familiarise themselves with the interface. In this respect, it's a bit like learning a new language: the key to understanding its syntax and quirks is to **immerse oneself and practice and practice and practice.**

2. That said, this kind of practice means a lot of trial and error. You have probably done similar, in private, with other Moodle tools. When I say 'in private' I mean that we can tinker with the system until we are **happy with the result, and then show it** to our students. In this instance, however, learning how Workshops function is only really possible when a group of participants –your students– is actively engaged with the system. Bear in mind that the tool generates part of the student's final mark (the thing your student really cares about). It follows that we do not enjoy the same flexibility to blithely learn from our mistakes as with other Moodle modules. There is something of a **Catch 22 at play**: to learn to use it, I need to make mistakes, but I can't afford to make mistakes because the grades are too important...

For these reasons, I have strived to set this text apart from the cold documentation that our institutions usually provide us with; and likewise the official documentation that Moodle itself provides. I have based the work on my experience, which I can divide into two strands. Firstly, this book draws heavily from the countless **hours I spent engaging in my own trial and error** while learning how to teach my students with Workshop. Secondly, working closely with other education professionals and delivering this course to them, I have been able to consider other viewpoints and uses of the tool that I would never have contemplated on my own.

Opportunities and advantages of Workshops

The main advantage is pedagogical. Of the six cognitive levels that we aim to stimulate in our students (Memorization, Comprehension, Application etc. see Bloom's taxonomy) it is generally accepted that Evaluation and Synthesis (creativity) are the closest to **'deep learning', and therefore, the most 'transformational'**. Research consistently shows that by engaging with peer-evaluation we not only learn 'more' but that we also learn 'better'. From time to time, when I'm at my desk assessing students' work, red pen in hand, I think to myself —and I'm sure I'm not the only one—: «*Oh, I wish all the students could see some of these! They could learn a lot from looking at these!*» In truth, at times it's while we are correcting students' work that we teachers learn the most. One day, teaching a class on Editing in Journalism, I arrived at a sad but undeniable conclusion: As 'formal-assessor' I was stockpiling, rather than sharing, my students' learning and was (not to put too fine a point on it) **robbing them** of a valuable learning opportunity. Workshops return to our students what is rightfully theirs.

The second key advantage is the impressive **scalability** of the tool. It's true, that organising a Workshop takes a significant amount of effort. But once it's done, using it with ten students, or one hundred, or one thousand doesn't really require much more. And if that was not enough, once you have created the Workshop, you can refine it and re-use it as many times as you like. In our teaching institutions, we are always being to design assessments that are at simultaneously formative, continuous and sustainable. Traditional continuous assessment, based on practical exercises tick the first two boxes but fail on the third: we have finite time and energy, and organising these exercises leaves us with a model that simply does not scale well. Nor are these exercises guaranteed to be applicable to multiple groups of students. In response to that institutional demand for 'real' assessment, almost without fail we give the same old replies: «*lack of resources, not enough time..., large numbers of students*» etc. Far from being limited by the size of the cohort, when we use Workshops, **the system actually becomes more reliable as the sample group grows**.

The third advantage I see is a little more subjective.

Much like Sisyphus pushing his boulder up the hill, after years and years of red-penning the same mistakes over and over, the teacher's vocation and enthusiasm can begin to feel a little stretched. The requirement to devise quality rubrics is the complete opposite of this drudgery. Systematizing those decisions that we typically take when assessing students presents **a constant series of intellectually fulfilling challenges**. We have all known colleagues who inhabit one or the other end of this spectrum. At one extreme, there are those who admirably sacrifice so much of themselves, rigorously completing each and every repetive task required of them. And at the other extreme are the non-conformists, motivated by the desire to innovate and the quest to discover the answer to the eternal question: «*How far can the rock climb the hill by itself before I need to start pushing?*»

Entire civilisations, let alone the educational establishment, have got this far thanks to the balance of citizens at both ends of that spectrum. For the reason that this book has ended up in your hands, it's likely you fall into the second camp.

Pre-requistes and Challenges

There are also pre-requisites or obstacles that have occasionally led to me advising against the use of Workshop to some teachers.

The first is that creating Workshops has to be seen as an incredibly profitable **investment** of time. But, of course, to invest it, you need to have it first. Trying to use Workshops as an emergency solution indicates that the teacher does not understand its functionality. The return on the investment on a Workshop starts, according to my own calculations, around the third or fourth time you use them. If we factor in the time that you are spending right now reading this book, we could even say the fifth time. Having said that, it is a guaranteed return on investment. Soon, you will be **spending three hours in work to achieve something that would once have taken you twenty**. Take my word for it.

The second is that the calculation of the final mark, and the control of the Workshop process requires a basic understanding of statistics. I am not suggesting that you need to be a professor of Algebra or an experienced poker player, but at the very least, you **can not be scared of percentages**. You need to be able to look at a big bucket of numbers and identify fairly quickly whether there are imbalances, obvious errors, or inverted tendencies.The functionality of Workshop is based on the idea that the larger the sample you provide, the more reliable the result. If you were to survey only two people on some topic, chance dictates that the result of such a scarce sample might not reflect reality. But when you ask the same question to twelve people instead, it is more likely that the answer tends to be reliable. For that same basic reason, it is much more advisable to run five so-so Workshops than try to run one perfect Workshop. This is one of the foundations that much of the following work is based on. If you are looking for a totally objective, infallible measuring tool, you should look elsewhere. Likewise, if you are someone with an allergy to data and statistics, you should close this book at this page, gift it to a colleague, and go back to your red pen.

The third barrier to entry are the **time constraints** of this type of group activity requires. Teachers are usually pretty flexible when it comes to submission of exercises, particularly when we are seeking to build good relationships with our students. So, rather than imposing a sanction —making a small reduction in the final mark for the piece, requiring a medical note etc.–, we usually let these things slide. Ultimately, we all need to get along; and as teachers we have an interest in maintaining a certain moral legitimacy and empathy with our students. The most challenging part of all is that our charges begin to take this for granted. The picture changes entirely when you entrust a machine to manage the logistics of student submissions. Imagine it like an airport. The boarding doors can perhaps stay open a minute or two for that tardy passenger, but once the plane has taken off, it's much more difficult for the plane to come back for them. In the case of Workshops, whether it is scheduled to run for two hours, two weeks or two months, there will be transition times, such as time to submit the exercise, or the peer-evaluation of classmates. These are configured beforehand and that will be contrary to the flexibility that both the student body and teacher are accustomed to.

Like a washing machine, once the wash has started, it is not nice to stop it and open the door for the sock you missed. There is a tension between the machine's strict workings and the more relaxed approach that humans tend to take. So, occasionally, you will need to make thankless decisions to exclude late submissions from the entire process (at least until the next wash). As before, my advice remains to run more frequent, smaller, Workshops. That way you can combine various scores to arrive at a mark, rather than just one make-or-break assessment and the the potential for drama that brings.

Another **difficulty you will face is designing good-quality rubrics**. This book explains the aspects of technical configuration and a set of best practices that you should follow to be successful. However, I'm afraid that that is the easiest part of the process. Homer Simpson once said that he only knew *«Three kinds of people; those who can count and those who cannot»*. Well, I only know two types of teacher: those who haven't designed a rubric yet, and those who know how difficult it is to design a good one. If you are still a member of the first group, I would urge you to join the second as soon as you can. And even though this is not a book about pedagogy, nor about measuring tools; nor does it claim any authority about the design of assessment rubrics; from the first chapter I will need to ask you that you edit at least one [see page 52] because it underpins absolutely everything else. Without a rubric, your Workshop has no foundations. It will be built on shifting sands. Really. Prepare your rubric first of all. If I could single out just one paragraph from this book to rescue from a burning building, it would be (without a shadow of a doubt) this one.

One final piece of bad news. If you haven't noticed already, your student cohort isn't going to be delighted to be marking their classmates' work. Even though you will be feeling a sense of deep professional satisfaction, implementing collaborative learning, touching upon that elusive 'deep learning' we've all heard about, *[blah, blah, blah]*; watch out. Your students are only going to hear one thing: 'more work to do...' End of story. If you hoped that running Workshops would improve your scores in student satisfaction surveys* bear in mind that your students may feel differently. It may draw suspicion from students: *«you're making us do your work for you»*. For this reason, we must continuously strive to give the opposite message. You must find a **strategy to communicate** very clearly

*If you are really looking to improve scores in these surveys, I recommend you read **The Presentation Secrets of Steve Jobs** by Carmine Gallo and **Brain Rules** by the neurologist John Medina. Our audience is in the classroom and these two books, though not specifically about teaching, caused a sea change in my approach to lecturing. What I picked up from these books worked from day one, but that is for another book...

that you, the teacher, takes the process as seriously as they do. Make it plain that, rather than abandoning your duties, it is in fact the complete opposite. Above all you will need to imagine the tasks from their perspective and try to understand the conflicting interests of all parties with a little empathy and sensitivity.

That said:

I assure you it pays off. You start a fascinating journey. After twenty years dedicated to teaching, sometimes more and sometimes less successful, I have discovered the computer-assisted co-evaluation workshops and now I feel that, for the first time, my time is indeed dedicated to building something really important and that it returns tangible results, week after week.

Where do I start?

So we start by *Adding an activity*. Just like when we want to publish any other type of document in our course, the starting point is to *Activate Edition* and then click *Add an activity or resource*.

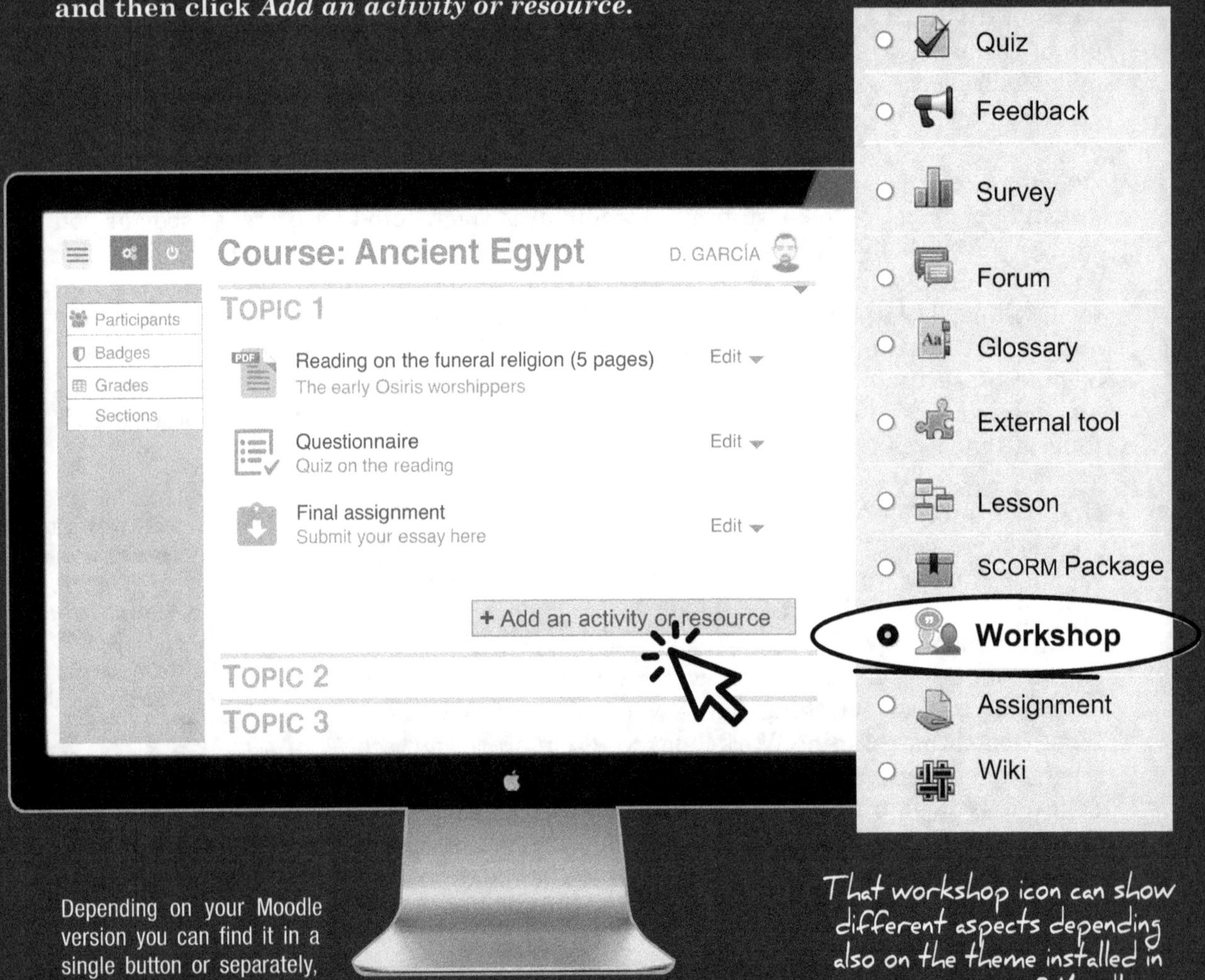

Depending on your Moodle version you can find it in a single button or separately, that is, on one hand 'Add a **resource**' -referred to those more static or passive elements, such as File, Folder, Label, Book, Page, URL- and, on the other, 'Add an **activity**' -these others do mobilize the students, force them to participate, answer or submit exercises, such as Tasks, Surveys, Quizzes, Discussion Forums, Polls, Wikis or like this one: the **Workshop**-.

That workshop icon can show different aspects depending also on the theme installed in your version of Moodle

Main Settings

Next, the ***Settings*** editing page (*Adding a New Workshop*) contains a dozen drop-down sections, some of which are already familiar to us because they are common to other Moodle resources —such as *General*, *Grading Settings*, *Availability*, *Access Restrictions*, etc.— Let's break them down one by one in the same order that they will appear on screen. To explore all the epigraphs it is usually more convenient to *Expand* them *all* beforehand.

Get familiar with this 'Expand all' / 'Collapse all' option, which with a simple click, conveniently displays all the subsections of **any menu page in Moodle**

All sections collapsed

All sections expanded

General

The *Workshop name* is the short title that your students will see on the course main page along with the rest of the resources of your subject, without any decorations or design, while the *Description* does admit editing of styles -bolds, italics, images, tables, links, etc.- and therefore it is optional whether it is **displayed** or not (lower box). Between the two of them they announce what is the workshop abotu. So they are not yet the 'instructions' for the submission, which will have their corresponding section later on.

My advice is that while the workshop is alive we show a brief description on the course page, to highlight its presence, otherwise it may go unnoticed when competing with the rest of your resources. One or two sentences will be enough describing what the workshop consists of or a small logo or image that identifies it. I recommend a verb in imperative tense – «*Answer here... Click here to hand in your homework...*».

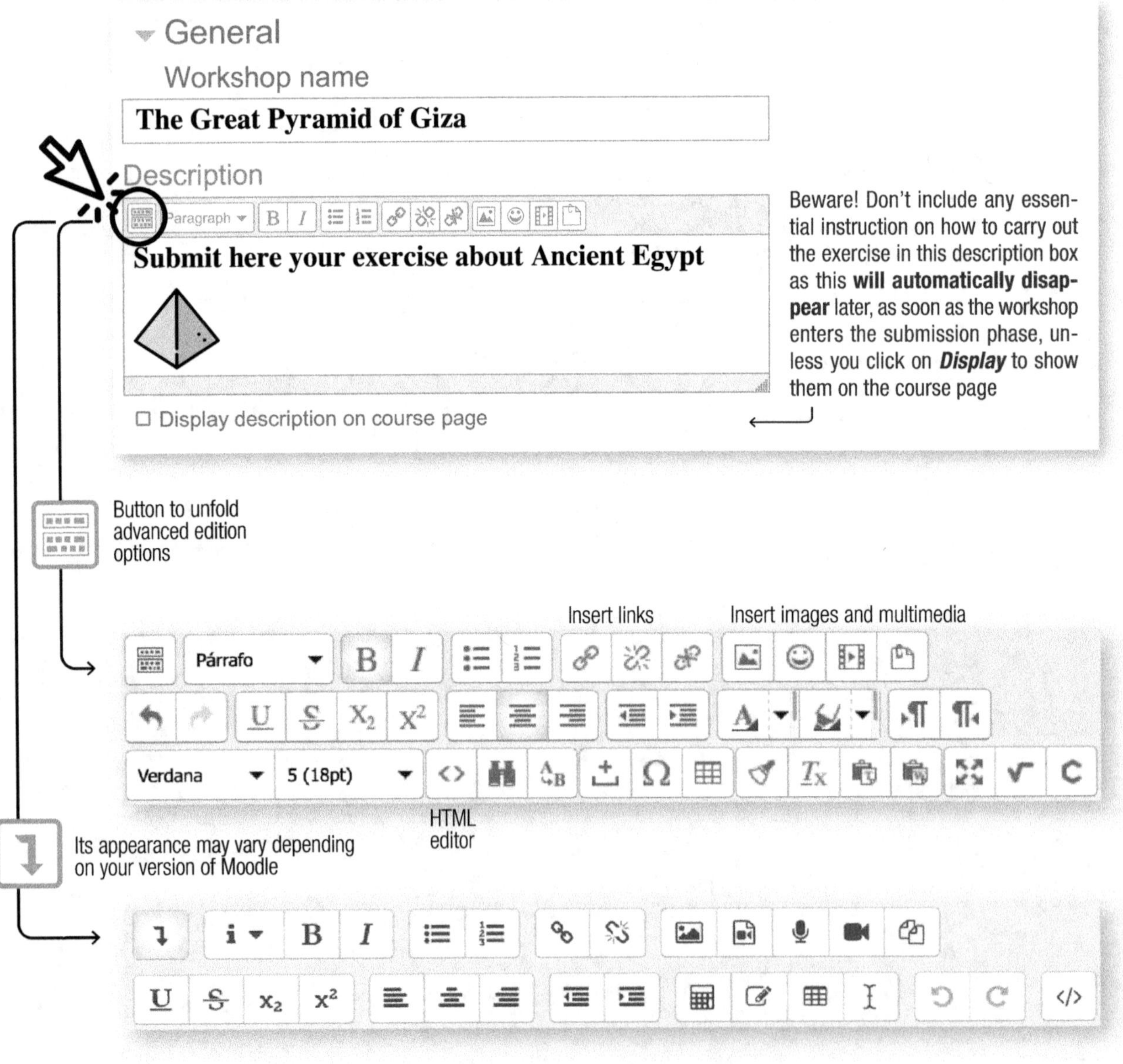

Grading settings

This section is vital. Here we make the first decisions that affect the essence of the workshop. The first one is to choose among the four possible *Grading strategies*. So decisive is this step that Moodle in its official documentation classifies the Workshop 'Types' —as it literally calls them— into four, according to these options. Throughout the book we will break them down. For now, it is important to know that your choice will be reduced from four to only two, so far. Because of the following reason:

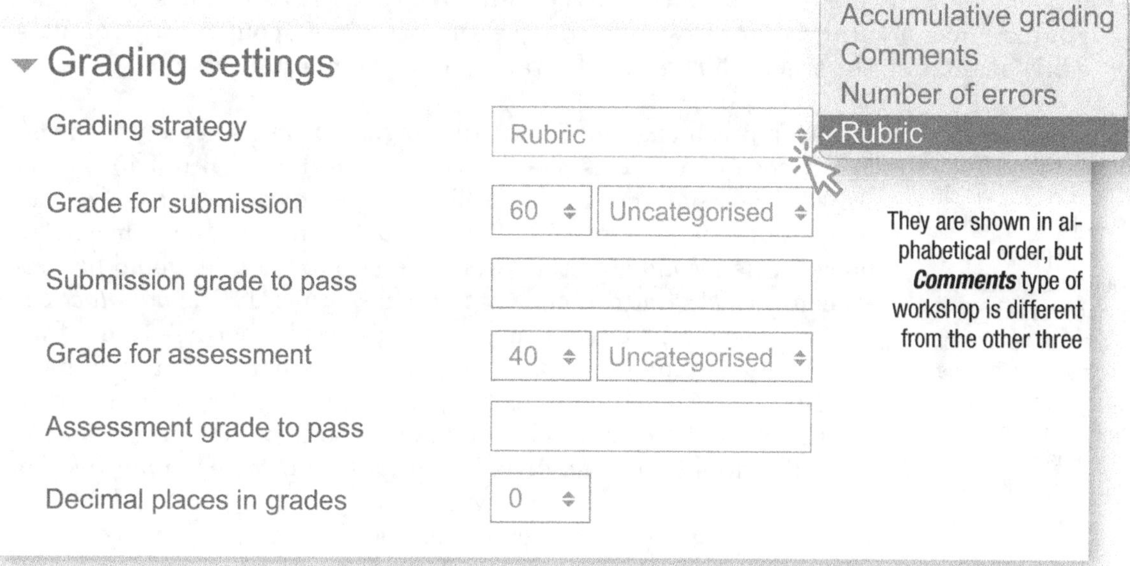

Although the four appear alphabetically in the drop-down list (A*cumulative grading, Comments, Number of errors* and *Rubric*) one of them is qualitatively different from the other three. This is the ***Comments*** type of the workshop, which consists of a workshop in which students **do not grade or give a numerical mark to their classmates**, but simply text-based feedback, advice and opinions to each other. In other words, everyone gets a 'full mark' (100%) for their mere participation. This is a great tool for group dynamics, but if we want this activity to return differentiated grades at the end, we will have to calculate them ourselves.

On the contrary, with the other three strategies we can design some evaluation forms for the students to review other people's work by means of scales (for example, *Good/Bad/Regular*), numerical scores (i.e., from 0 to 5) and a list of possible errors (*Yes/No*).

Until you get familiar with the three strategies that do involve rating, I advise starting with the '***Rubric***'. In addition, this one is so versatile that it allows us to adapt and function like the other two, which are somewhat more limited

Although we are deciding on an essential feature of the workshop, it turns out that it is possible to **change the grading strategy later**, on the fly, even after submissions or evaluation phase. That is, we could set up the workshop first as a cross-feedback forum (*Comments*) and after the students have submitted, reviewed and shared their opinions, go back and allow them to modify their own exercises in the light of those comments received and convert the workshop to *Rubric* format. But first you must master its different *Phases*, which we will see shortly.

And how many points will the submission be worth and how many points will the assessment of others be worth?

Then, by means of the *Grade for Submission* and *Grade for the assessment*, we will decide the mark we want to give to that exercise submitted (from 0 to 100) and to the other task of reviewing the others' exercises (again from 0 to 100), respectively. In order to calculate it, I usually pay attention to the estimated time that each phase will take. For example, if I think that answering the question will take about twenty minutes while evaluating the others thirty, then I award 2 and 3 points respectively.

We are also free to choose 20 and 30 (without decimals) or 2 and 3 with one decimal, which would be similar. Personally, I prefer this second option: Carrying out more workshops throughout the course and giving a very low number of points to each one, so that the students **perceive that in each workshop they are only risking a few tenths of a grade**. This reassures them and relaxes the whole process

If you find it more convenient to imagine them as percentages you can choose two figures that add up to one hundred (60/40, 20/80, 0/100). Note that both tasks could be scored indistinctly from zero to one hundred (and they would add up to 200 in total), or from zero to one (in this second case they would add up to 2 and it would be convenient to add some decimals with the lower menu: *Decimal places in grades*). However, for convenience, choose a numbering system that adapts later to the rest of the exercises or evaluations that you have announced in your course. If this particular workshop is going to be worth 15% of their final grade, it will also be easier for the student to imagine those 15 tenths distributed like that (for example five for their answer and ten for reviewing others', or *viceversa*) and for you to make the subsequent calculations, of course.

Now, if you already use the Moodle *Gradebook* and you are using it to automatically compile the aggregates of their different assignments —or you plan to do so in the future— or you simply share the teaching along with other instructors who request different practices, then it is appropriate for you, for convenience, that these two figures move in the same **order of magnitude** as the rest of the exercises.

Let's say at the beginning of the course you asked them to do a short task of a few minutes and you scored it from zero to ten. Now, to maintain proportionality with the next workshop, which, let's say, will take them seven times that time, it would be good to score it from zero to seventy (for example 20/50) and thus save you the effort of having to recalculate the partial weights later.

In a few days, when you close the workshop and end it, Moodle will show these two figures to the participants. Like this.

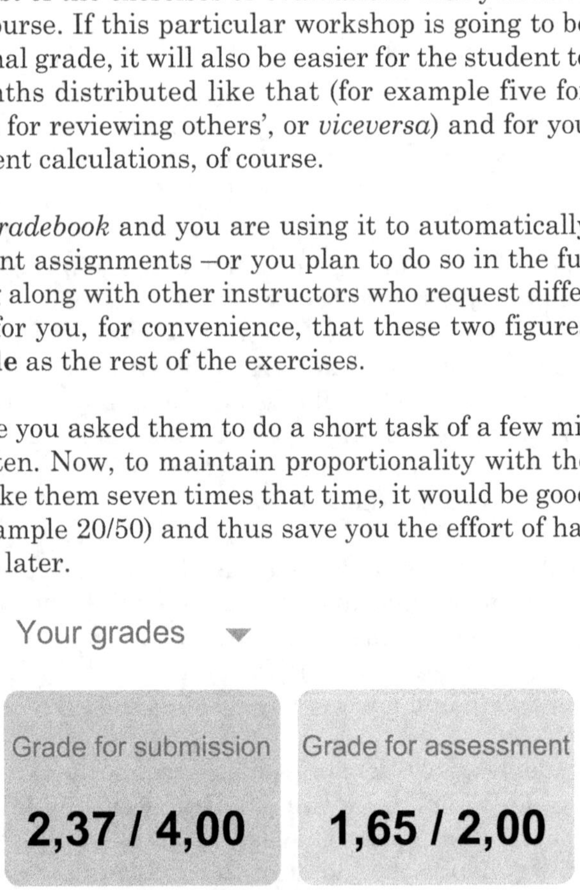

To each participant their two grades: each one next to the total on which it is calculated

The so-called **pass** and **fail** grades only work internally in Moodle, e.g. to allow to link up of activities in a specific sequence and to make it a condition to have passed this one in order to be able to access another one in the future. Each of the two tasks (*Submission* and *Assessment*) are passed separately, as two completely independent activities with their own bar. You can leave both sections at '0' and wait for another time to update this parameter.

All Moodle activities and resources offer this interesting option called '**Access restrictions**'. It allow us to establish the order in which the contents are seen or to filter which users can or cannot access them at any time

Finally, the drop-down menu on the right –*Uncategorised*– would allow us to select one of the categories that we may have previously divided our Moodle *Gradebook* into, so that we can choose which one to assign each of the grades to. If there are no categories in your course yet this drop-down will simply be empty.

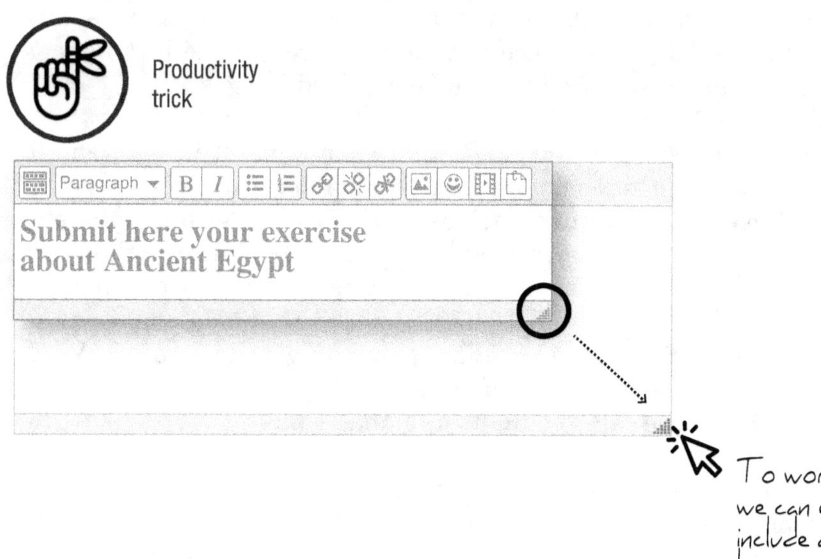

To work more comfortably we can extend the boxes that include a striped triangle in its lower corner **by dragging it**

Submission settings:

Here we will finally write the instructions for the task. Unlike the *Description*, which was limited to announcing or summarizing the workshop, in this other field we must introduce all the necessary indications for them to understand what we are asking for, since it will be what the students see on the submission screen. The instructions can range from a brief «*Answer here to the question asked yesterday in the classroom*» – which would be referring to guidelines provided beforehand– to detailed instructions that provide reading documents, links to external websites, videos, PDFs, etc. All the material that the student may later need to prepare his/her answer. However, two things should be kept in mind:

1. Along with the instructions for sending, and regardless of how short or long they are, it is also always advisable to announce –just briefly–, what the **evaluation criteria** will be afterwards. Because if we did not describe them beforehand the student would only know them during the next phase, that of *Evaluation*, when it may already be late. Explaining briefly how much each criterion will be worth afterwards will help to guide the student in their work, to finish off our instructions, to motivate them and to avoid possible frustrations or misunderstandings. In addition, it will accustom the participants to better understand the rubric that later they will have to use to evaluate their classmates.

2. Beware! Although in this *Description* field we can format our text with links to other websites, design attributes such as colours, bold type, tables, etc. surprisingly the **images** we embed are very likely NOT to be seen. This is a bug that Moodle has not solved in some versions. You should check it in yours. It's a pity, since it would have been the ideal place to be able to present the instructions with the greatest possible visual richness and embedded images.

The *Maximum number of submission attachments* that each student may attach to their submission is seven. Normally one is more than enough, but the most advisable option is **to leave out these attachments entirely**. Whenever possible, an online text submission will be preferable to a file, since, let's remember, not only are they sending them to us, but they will be received by all of the participants and if we do not use standard formats (such as JPG, PDF, MP3, MP4 etc.), some of the students may not be able to access the files because of the corresponding paid software (Microsoft Word, Excel, Photoshop, Powerpoint) or their latest version, or it may be impossible to save it in a compatible format, etc. These cases could be unmanageable.

Therefore, when the task can be summarized in a few paragraphs, it is convenient to let the number of attached files be '**zero**' and thus concentrate the answers on the screen, instead of relying on files that would have to be downloaded separately. In addition, their on-screen submission box supports **rich text**, which means that it already accepts the insertion of images, external links, etc. without any need to rely on external files.

▾ Submission settings

Instructions for submission

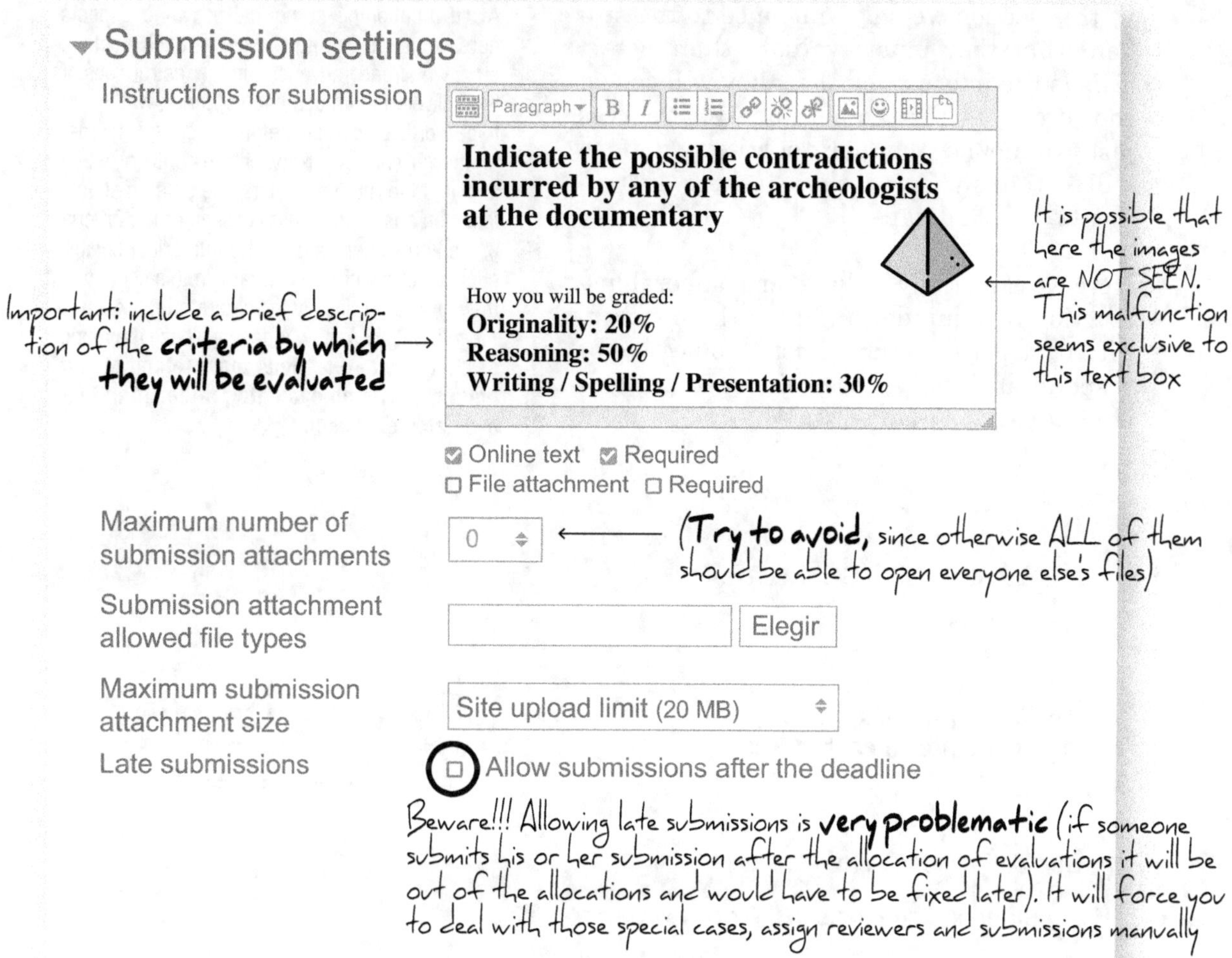

Maximum number of submission attachments

Submission attachment allowed file types

Maximum submission attachment size

Late submissions

*Important: include a brief description of the **criteria by which they will be evaluated***

It is possible that here the images are NOT SEEN. This malfunction seems exclusive to this text box

*(**Try to avoid**, since otherwise ALL of them should be able to open everyone else's files)*

*Beware!!! Allowing late submissions is **very problematic** (if someone submits his or her submission after the allocation of evaluations it will be out of the allocations and would have to be fixed later). It will force you to deal with those special cases, assign reviewers and submissions manually*

Below we can indicate the format or formats of files that are allowed to be attached, their maximum size in MegaBytes (which will be limited to the one imposed by the website administrator for the teachers. In my university, for example, it is 20 MB).

Finally, the option of allowing or not allowing late submissions serves to accept late deliveries that either took longer than the deadline or were submitted during the next phase, the evaluation phase. But think twice about it, because if we activate this, that is, if we are lax with them, then we will have to be very attentive to whether or not they arrive on time to the allocations phase, because otherwise they could remain in limbo (no exercises assigned to evaluate and no evaluators in charge of reviewing theirs). So we would need to manually assign them both those tasks to be reviewed and select other reviewers to evaluate theirs.

Assessment settings:

In this section we only announce to the student that they must evaluate their peers. This is the information that they will see on the screen during the next phase. It serves just to announce the rubric or criteria that we will establish later –those others instruments, yes, in detail–.

Here we can briefly include some general instruction or reminder and take the opportunity to insist that they must be objective or respond as fairly as possible since **part of their grade is also at stake**.

Avoid mentioning numerical or rating aspects here (what percentage is worth each section, etc.). We already advanced in the instructions of the delivery how much each criterion was going to be worth. It was said before we started in order to answer correctly. Now, on the contrary, when applying the rubric to others, the student should focus on answering what is asked or the criteria presented rather than on the numerical consequences of his choices. In fact, in this section of the workshop I usually indicate a brief: «*Answer the following correctly*» (and then I pose the rubric as a **battery of questions that pretend to test him or her, as an evaluator, rather than that evaluated exercise**).

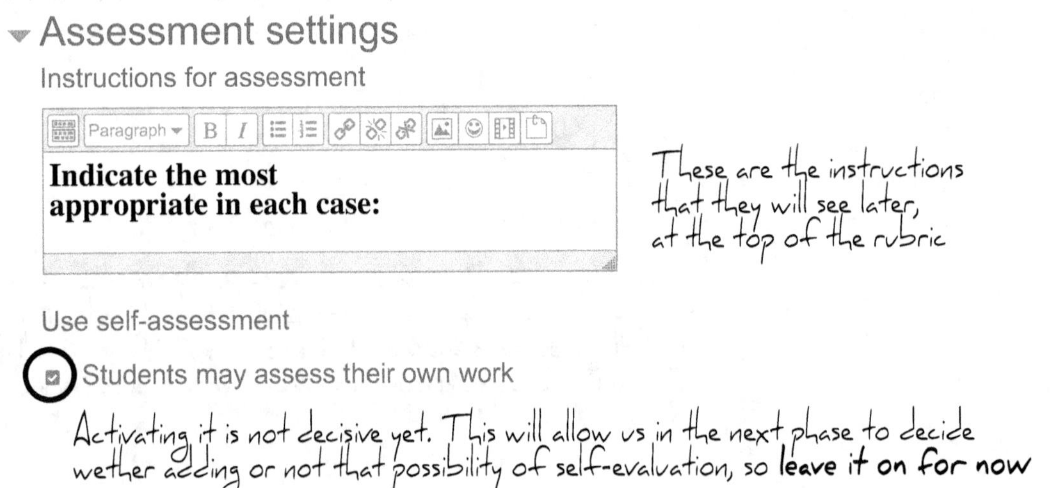

In the next box –*Use self-evaluation*– we only choose whether or not we will later allow participants to correct their own exercise as well. We are not yet deciding, but simply leaving that possibility open for later, in the *Allocation* phase. We don't understand why Moodle commits this redundancy, as where we will actually set it up will be later, when we make the allocations. So for the moment my advice here is to leave it on in any case.

Feedback

Under this heading Moodle mixes quite diverse parameters. Firstly, the *Overall feedback mode*, which serves to add a text box to the assessment screen so that students, after reviewing an exercise, can add **a personal explanation** in free text format at the end to be read by the assessed colleague. The three options are *Enabled and Optional* (they can add such comments if they wish), *Enabled and required* (they must write something in this field in order to submit their assessments) and *Disabled*.

Note that enabling this type of final comments may be of interest only if the evaluators have not been able to express their subjective opinions during the evaluation phase itself (as happens when filling in the headings or giving the numerical grades of the *Acumulative Grading*, where they have merely responded to closed forms and have not been able to freely qualify or provide their feedback). However, this possibility contributes very little in case the evaluation strategy selected has already been simply *Comments*, because, as we have seen, in that other type of workshop the students **will already have been writing their opinions continuously** through free text fields.

Enabling this final 'Conclusion' can be very productive and enriching when we are sure that the students will really make valuable contributions. But let's keep in mind that in other cases allowing this direct feedback can also serve to **open a can of worms** by encouraging the crossing of subjective opinions that only demonstrate the disparity of criteria or result in the delegitimization of the peer-evaluation process.

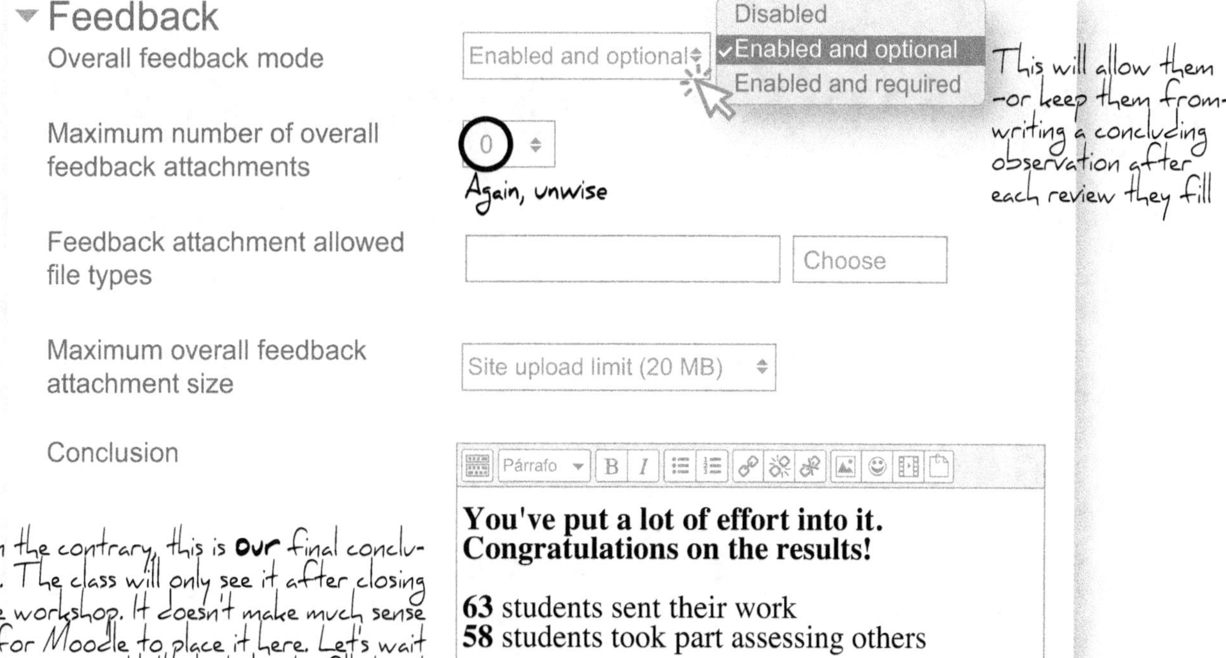

This will allow them —or keep them from— writing a concluding observation after each review they fill

Again, unwise

On the contrary, this is **our** final conclusion. The class will only see it after closing the workshop. It doesn't make much sense for Moodle to place it here. Let's wait until the last day to fill it out

Next, the option: *Maximum number of overall feedback attachments* is designed for the case that this feedback between reviewers and reviewees is delivered by means of a file (such as comments glossed to a PDF or a Powerpoint, or with a photograph, text file, audio recordings, etc.), in which case we can limit the format of the admitted files and, again, their maximum size.

It is enough here to remember those possible technical complications, commented above, that this can cause. I personally advise against it again unless the nature of the exercise requested (an audio, a video, etc.) makes it essential.

Finally, in the *Conclusion* section, the teacher can write his or her own overall feeling about the activity, referring to the whole class, which will only be public to the participants once the workshop is closed. Visit the chapter dedicated to the *Closing* of the workshop where you will find some important observations about what other information is very convenient to include in this field.

For example, in this final *Conclusion* I like to indicate the total number of people who have participated, the overall satisfaction of the activity, a motivation to participate in the next one, etc. We can also leave it empty. However, **there is no logical reason for Moodle to place here, in this section of the *Setup***, a conclusion that, as its name suggests, should be the last thing the teacher fills in and the participants discover.

Example submissions

This option –at first glance, so interesting– allows teachers to exhibit exercises as a sample so that students can train in the evaluation of potential answers before proceeding with the real ones, those of their classmates. In this case we will have to construct or provide these fictitious exercises as examples (for example, because there are cases of correct or very wrong answers respectively or because they shine in some aspect or, on the contrary, they lack what is requested). Then we proceed to evaluate them ourselves so that they serve as a sample for the students, who will be able to try to judge them without this influencing their grade as evaluators. This kind of previous training can be compulsory or optional. But since **these finished exercises could often give clues about the solution to the exercise or, worse, limit the creativity requested** in the instructions, the third option in the drop-down menu is more interesting: that these examples only appear «*After having sent your own task and before evaluating other people's tasks*».

The fact is that it would often be impossible for us to construct examples of possible responses without revealing the solution or without clearing the ground that we are precisely asking them to discover on their own.

▼ Example submissions

If we prepare pre-evaluated sample exercises for practice, here we will select whether it is voluntary or mandatory to evaluate them and whether we prefer to be shown before or after submitting

Use examples	☐ Example submissions are provided for practice in assessing
Mode of examples assessment	Voluntary | Compulsory before submitting | After submitting ⬍

Those three options are:

- *Assessment of example submissions is voluntary*
- *Examples must be assessed before own submission*
- *Examples are available after own submission and must be assessed before peer assessment*

Regardless of whether we select one or the other, we can only upload these sample submissions to the workshop during the *Configuration* phase. In the control panel a new indication will appear: *'Example submissions'* 'and in the lower area the button *Add example submission*. The dialog box that we will fill in to upload them emulates the one that the students will also use later. And after completing it a confirmation box will warn us that «...*You have to assess this example submission to provide a reference assessment...*».

Availability

These options refer to temporary scheduling. The opening and closing deadlines for receiving exercises are already familiar to us, as they are common to other Moodle tasks and resources. However, time management in the Workshops is a bit more complicated for the following **three reasons**:

Firstly, if we want to automate the opening and closing deadlines (with the corresponding *Enable* box on the right) we see that **both appear duplicated,** as they are considered for all purposes as two different and successive tasks. Thus, we can assign the submission its own opening or closing date/time (or both) and also the assessment its own opening and/or closing deadlines.

Secondly, please note that the workshop **does not automatically enter the *Submission phase*** even if we allow an opening time here to accept these deliveries. Students will only be able to do so when we **manually** move the workshop to that phase. In other words, although the appearance of this menu may suggest that we are programming a start time for the task submission, the starting shot will only be given when we click on *Switch to the next phase*, as we will see in the section dedicated to the temporary management of the workshop.

This can be a bit frustrating. In my first experiences with the temporary programming of workshops, it happened to me that after enabling this deadline for accepting submissions, **I was calm and convinced that I had started the activity, when it was not the case**. Until a student told me that it was impossible for them to submit assignments, I didn't realize that I must have manually advanced to the *Submission phase* by clicking on it.

Do not mistake the **opening date** for submissions with the start of the 'Submission Phase'. The starting pistol must ALWAYS be fired manually. The workshop does not enter into submission phase even if we have this date enabled, be careful

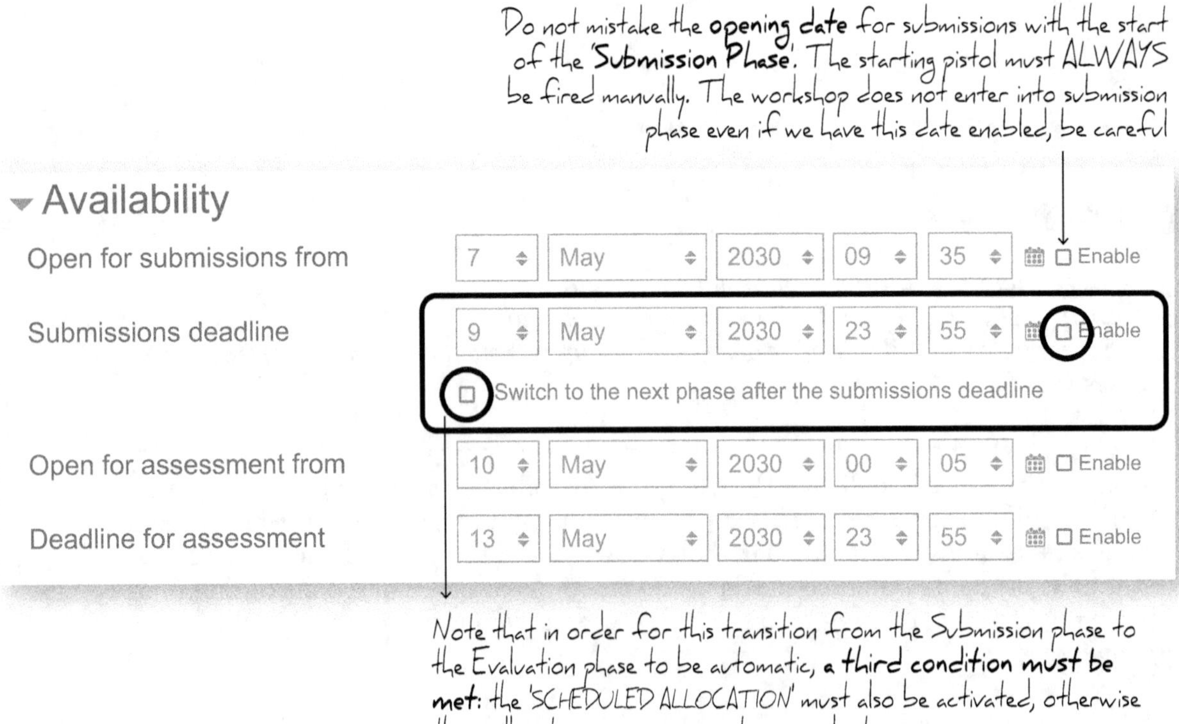

Note that in order for this transition from the Submission phase to the Evaluation phase to be automatic, a **third** condition **must be met**: the 'SCHEDULED ALLOCATION' must also be activated, otherwise they will not see any exercises to co-evaluate.

Thirdly, although the option *Switch to the next phase after the submissions deadline* may be very suggestive (of course, if I have set a deadline for the delivery phase, why not accept them directly to evaluate the colleagues from that moment, right?), well, because in practice this automated jump between phases will only happen if a third planet is also aligned: **that we have also programmed as 'automatic' another intermediate phase** and that it is not mentioned there –**that of *Allocate submissions*–**.

We will later see how that's kind of a bridge phase, in which the exercises are assigned across the participants and which, curiously, is then configured on a different screen. From here we still do not have access to it.

Consecuently, for these three reasons and until you do not feel comfortable with the temporary programming of the deadlines, my advice is not to touch any of these options and to control the progress of each phase of the workshop manually on the day that the date or time you have chosen arrives.

Common module settings

Through the *Availability* section –as with any other Moodle Resource or Activity– the workshop can also be shown or hidden from students.

The *ID number* of any Moodle resource is kind of its registration number. As teachers create contents, their ID is automatically generated as consecutive numbers that also appear in the visible URL, i.e. in your browser's address bar. It will be rare that we need or want to modify it to manually assign another one. So let's skip to the next section, which is going to be vital.

In recent versions of Moodle you will see a third intermediate option entitled ***Available but not shown on course page*** which allows us to keep it hidden but allow access to it via its direct link (URL). This option, although is interesting for other resources, is less useful for workshops.

Common module settings

Availability	Shown| Hidden| Available but not shown on course
ID number	
Group mode	No groups
	✓ No groups
	Separate groups
	Visible groups
Grouping	None
	Add group/grouping access restrictions

With 'No groups' there will be no boundaries between them (all together / totum revolutum). If there are 'Separate groups', those in one group will not evaluate exercises from the others. And 'Visible groups' allows the opposite, they will co-evaluate only to members of other groups, not of one's own

This is the *Group mode*, through which we can allow an «all with all» –*No groups* option, and thus anyone can evaluate anyone– or, on the contrary, limit the activity of each participant in this workshop to exclusively the group of which he or she is a part –with *Separate groups*–.

If your Moodle does not allow changes in this section, the reason may be that the group mode is *Forced* from the course settings. You can change it from the home page: ***Edit settings/Edit course settings/Groups/Do not force group mode***

The third option –*Visible groups*– makes possible an intermediate solution: that each participant can evaluate any other **except precisely those with whom he shares a group**. But this last decision is not yet made here. We will see later that it is in the *Allocation* phase where we can finally establish it. But, to do it there, we must have opened that possibility here, with visible Groups.

Now, whether your students are classified in groups or not is something that you must have configured previously, at the level of your course, from the *Course settings* section. If you haven't done so yet, check the *Participants* menu. It is possible to have them divided, for example, into a morning and an afternoon group. If you are interested in having each one evaluating only exercises from their own group you would activate the option *Separate groups*.

Also from the course main page you can change the group mode with a simple click on this little icon on the right. This, more than handy, **seems to be a real danger**, because **if we click it by mistake** this essential aspect of the workshop will be modified.

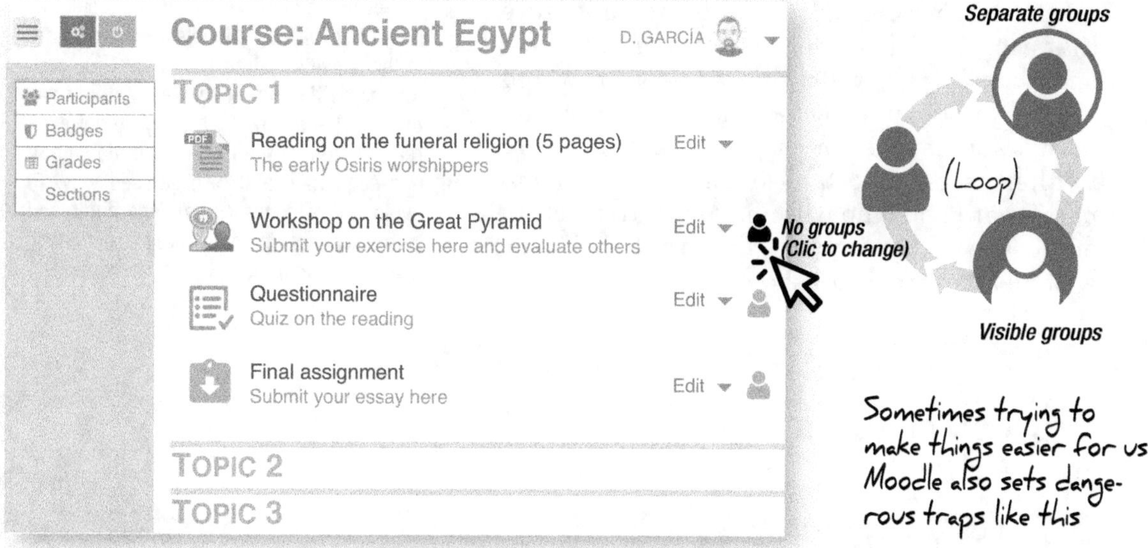

One of the most attractive features of the peer-evaluation workshops, and one that I am most often asked about by other teachers, is that the students themselves can evaluate the individual contribution of each of their classmates to **an exercise completed among several students**. As we have mentioned, it is essential to activate here the option *Separate groups* and – to avoid the cumbersome task of having to create a large number of small groups ourselves – very useful to have installed in our Moodle an optional plugin called *Group self-selection*, developed by three computer scientists from the Finnish Technological University of Tampere.

Thanks to the free module *Group self-selection* I delegate the creation and management of groups to my students. You can install it from: **https://moodle.org/plugins/ mod_groupselect**

Finally, Moodle calls the higher, broader categories *Groupings*, which we can also create to cover, in turn, *Groups*. Again, this is managed at the course level beforehand.

For example, my students of the 'Morning Shift' are in turn subdivided into three groups according to their surname, hence I decided to create two groups – one called Afternoon and one called Morning – and, again, **within the latter, the three separate** groups.

Restrict access:

One of the most interesting features of Moodle is to restrict access to any resource or
activity depending on the fulfilment of some condition. For example, having previously
participated in another activity or having obtained a certain minimum grade in a previous one, belonging to a certain group or —on the contrary— not belonging to any or
not having participated in a specific previous activity... etc. This ensures that throughout the course the students have passed each exercise or received the materials, done
the readings or answered the quizzes in a specific sequential order, not in a way that
each and every one would like.

These access restrictions are extremely versatile
and useful. For example: if I want to make sure
that each participant has downloaded the PDF
on Ancient Egypt, watched a video or answered
a short questionnaire before they can participate
in this workshop, I can set those conditions here
to filter users and establish who will be able to
participate and who will not. Or, better yet, to
encourage the latter to comply with them if they
wish to access the workshop.

In the case of regulated teaching, teachers
see every day how many students only remember to visit the Moodle or to participate
in the activities **when they count for grades or on the eve of the respective deadlines**. This means that many do not even
read the rest of the materials or do so in a
non-sequential and disorganised way. To
avoid this, *Access restrictions* combined
with *End of activity* control are two extremely
useful tools that are very easy to set up.

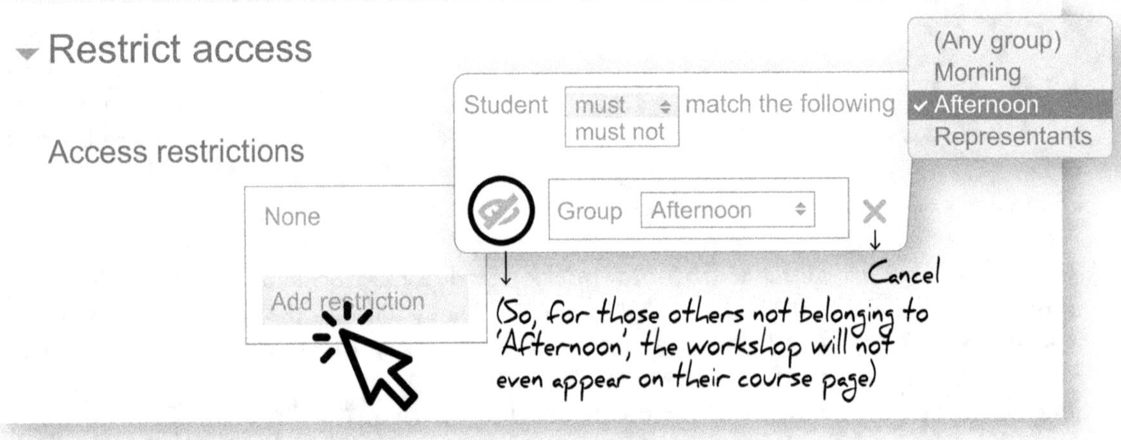

We have added this 'per group' access restriction so that
only the students in the afternoon group see the workshop and for the rest it does not even show up (to do
this: click on the eye and it will be crossed out)

This access restriction therefore serves as a filter so that some can enter to participate
in the workshop and others cannot. Unlike the *Group mode* that we have seen in the
previous section and that served to control **how the workshop itself will behave
with the participants once they are inside**. Don't confuse one with the other

Activity completion:

Closely linked to the previous one, this last section will only appear if in the course configuration you have activated the *Enable completion tracking* option, which serves to link in order some modules with others. If this is the case, students will see a small grey checkbox to the right of each assignment you put on the course main page, each document you upload or each quiz you prepare for them. This box tells them whether they have passed each assignment or not and what we do from this menu is to configure what 'pass' means, as it can be simply clicking, or downloading, or going to the end of the quiz, or receiving any grade, etc.

In the case of the workshops, as with all Moodle activities, this 'passing' of the activity can be done by the student themselves, either by clicking on it, or by receiving a grade ('finish').

If you are used to combining an activity with the next one in your class by means of the above-mentioned *Access restrictions*, it is essential to enable this option in the previous one –the one that will be a condition for access to this workshop– or in this same workshop if it is to be a condition for access, later, to any other.

This would allow us to link the workshop to future activities (for example, if participating in this workshop would later be a condition for accessing other content)

Activity completion

Completion tracking	Do not indicate | Manually mark | Only when conditions are met
Require view	☐ Student must view this activity to complete it
Require grade	☐ Student must receive a grade to complete this activity
Expect completed on	12 ⬍ May ⬍ 2020 ⬍ 23 ⬍ 55 ⬍ ☐ Enable

Save and return to course · **Save and display** · Cancel

And remember that it is not enough to 'Save changes and display' for participants to start sending their exercises. We will need to move manually to the 'Submission Phase' in any case.

You can now press **Save and display** to access, for the first time, the workshop's world famous **Control Panel**.

The control panel

Get acquainted with this table as soon as possible as we will control the workshop times from it

1
Setup

2
Submission

3
Allocate

Workshop: The Great Pyramid of Giza

Setup phase
Current phase

✔ Set the workshop description

✔ Provide instructions for submission

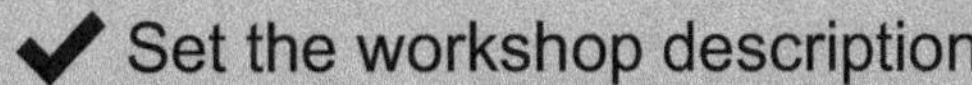

✘ Edit assessment form

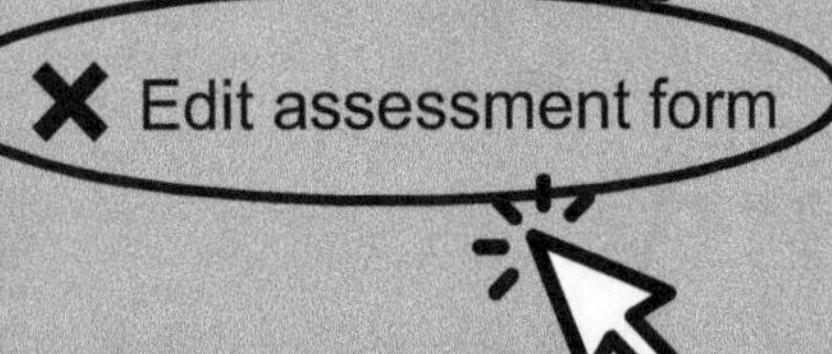

Submission phase
Switch to the submission phase

✔ Provide instructions for assessment

✘ Allocate submissions
Expected: 103
Submitted: 78
Allocated: 0

ⓘ There is at least one author who has not yet submitted their work

ⓘ Submissions deadline: Thursday 9 May 2030

4
Assessment

5
Grading

Edit settings
Locally assigned roles
Check permissions
Filters
Logs

Assessment phase
Switch to the assessment phase ○

Grading evaluation
Switch to the evaluation phase ○

Closed
Close workshop ○

✖ **Assess peers**
Total: 78
Pending: 78

ⓘ Assessment deadline :
Monday 13 May 2030

✖ **Calculate submission grades**
Expected: 103
Calculated: 0

✖ **Calculate assessment grades**
Expected: 103
Calculated: 0

✔ **Provide a conclusion of the activity**

The Workshop Control Panel is a five-section table that will accompany us throughout the process. It will allow us to carry out some fundamental actions:

Corroborate what stage we are at, as it is highlighted by a **different tone**, to ensure that the participants are indeed seeing what we think they are seeing at each moment.

Change from one stage to another, because although we saw that some of these jumps can be automated, this is the menu through which we will **move forward or backward** from one stage to another most of the time

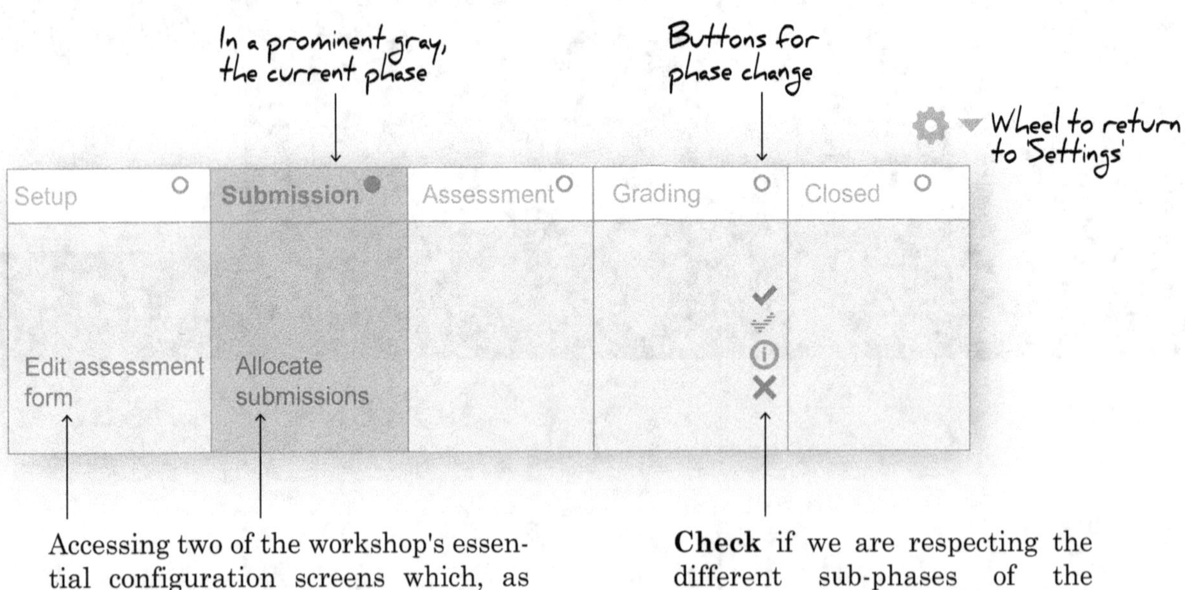

Accessing two of the workshop's essential configuration screens which, as you may have noticed, we have not yet been able to design. These are the *Assessment Form* and *Allocate Submissions*, which can only be reached from here.

Check if we are respecting the different sub-phases of the workshop at all times by means of this set of coloured icons with which Moodle alerts us.

From now on, we're going to go over what happens in each of the phases. The students will be the real protagonists of the second and the fourth —*Submission* and *Assessment*— while in the other three we will be able to work and make tests and adjustments privately until the result convinces us and we decide to move on to the next one.

Setup

Teachers:

We set up the basics of the workshop. None of them are definitive, we can come back here whenever we want and modify them, **even step into phase 2 so that they can deliver in the meantime** and we can keep setting this up

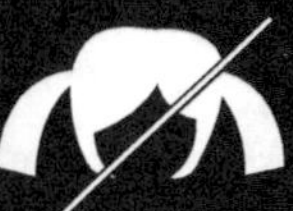

Students:

Opaque phase for them. They only see the 'Title', the 'Description' and a short message: *"The workshop is being set up"*

1. Setup phase

Wait a minute... If it turns out that this first phase is called *Setup*, then **what have we been doing so far?**

Well, that previous screen where we have been developing the workshop was the *Settings* screen. When we want to go back to it, we must look for the option *Edit Settings* in the upper configuration wheel. We could also go back by clicking on *Set the workshop description* or even on *Provide instructions for submission.*

Moodle seems to forget about the effort it takes to suddenly become familiar with dozens of new names for boring headings and menus. It invents several shortcuts to get to the same section. So, using any of these three menus, **you will end up returning to exactly the same** main *Settings* screen.

Therefore, these first two menus of the first tab or *Configuration Phase* refer us to two sections that we could already fill in when we started the workshop. They appear again in this list to remind us visually, **with a green or red color, if we have completed them or not**.

The third one, on the contrary, is new: *Edit assessment form*. This is, finally, the moment when we will be able to build the grid or list of evaluation criteria. Let's get to it:

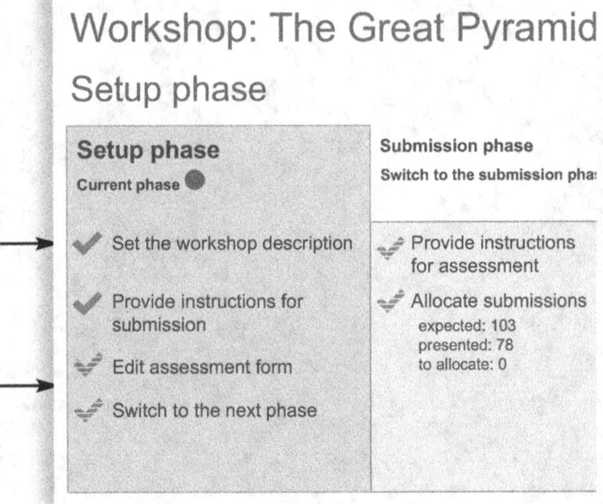

Editing assessment form:

Remember that when you had to choose between those four possible **Grading Strategies** – *Acumulative grading, Comments, Number of Errors* and *Rubric*– I strongly advised the latter.

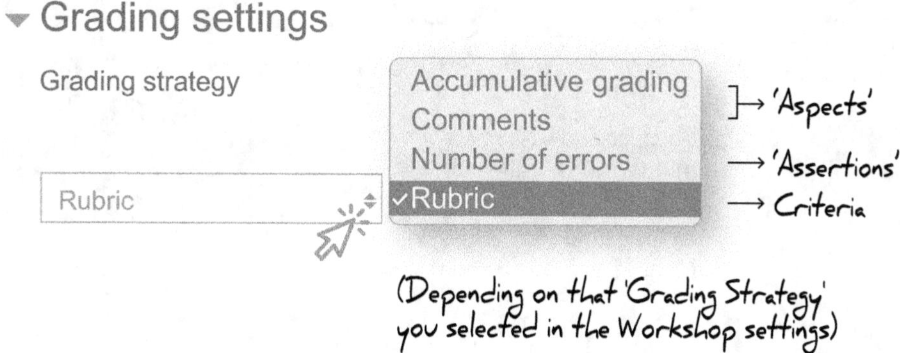

Now it is our responsibility to design a bunch of reviewing **Aspects**, **Assertions** or **Criteria** and write them clearly so that later it is intuitive for participants to judge other people's submissions.

Each one of these sections in which the evaluation is divided will have its own weight in the final grade –and it should respect the one we already warned participants about from the beginning of the exercise. That information we wrote in the *Submission settings*–.

We are going to go through all those four possible grading strategies one by one, although while we are setting them up, **nothing prevents us from advancing the workshop to the second phase** –*Submission*– **so that the students can start preparing and submitting their exercices** while we devote ourselves to this creative task. It would only be essential to have this evaluation sections completed in order to move on to the third phase –*Assessment*–, of course.

And remember that the most recommended habit is to have the structure, writing and scores of this rubric **prepared in advance**. In fact, as a precaution and thinking about potential future re-utilisation of the activity, if you lose or delete the workshop by mistake this would be the most valuable and most expensive information to recover, your rubric.

1. *Accumulative grading* form

Students must judge others' answers on each of these *Aspects* by awarding a **numerical** score or by predefined **scales**.

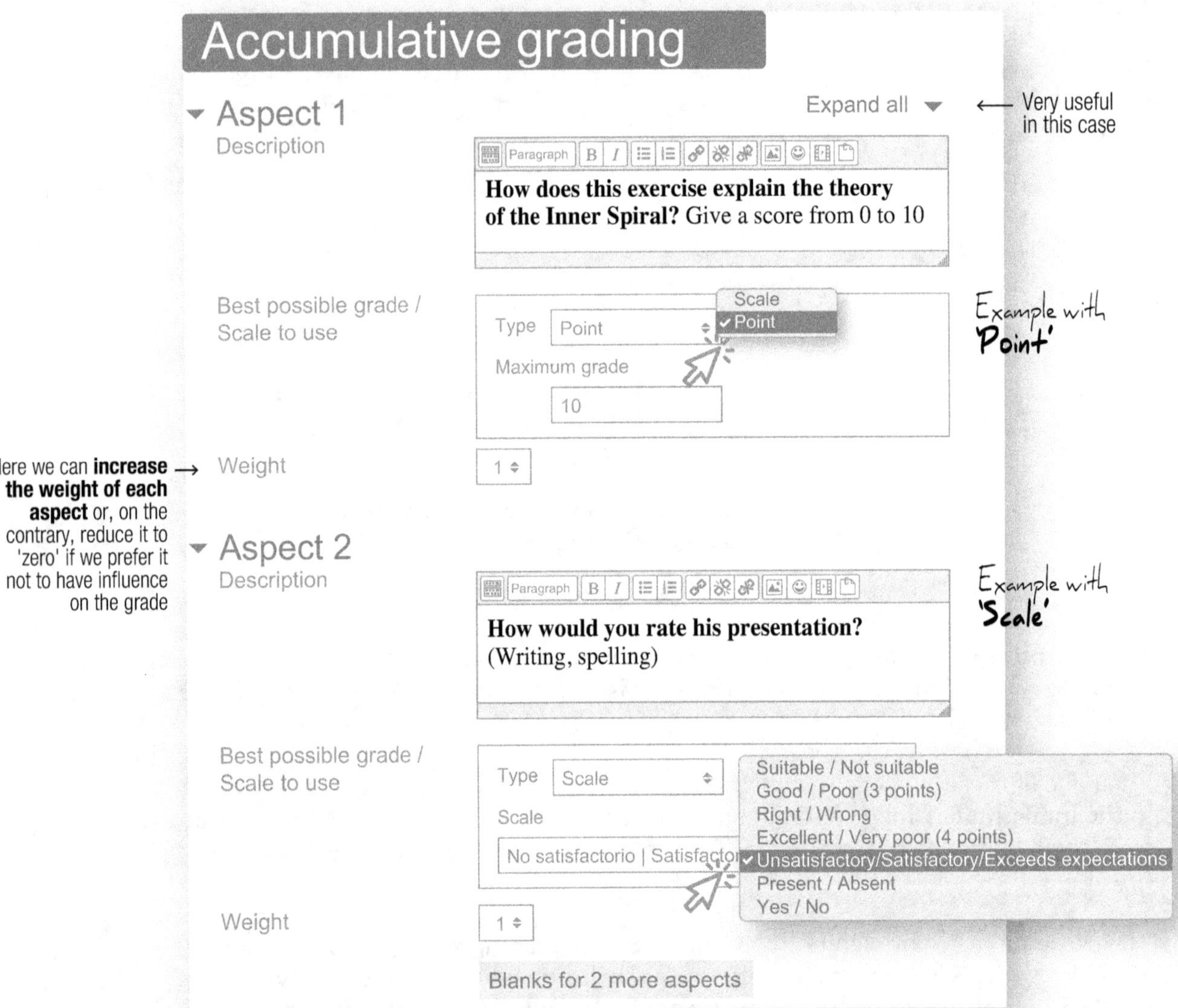

Note that here, when weighting, we are **not awarding 'points'** directly to each section, but only balancing their respective relative weights against each other. Remember that the points that were worth both the *Submission* and the *Assessment* are **already set** in the *Grade settings* section.

Let's say we establish three aspects. They would all have the same value (expressed as 'Weight 1' each) and weigh the same on the final note, 33% (and if we added a fourth, they would automatically be worth 25% each). If, on the other hand, we want any one of them to have half the weight of the other two, we could assign them 2, 2 and 1 respectively, which would make them weigh 40, 40 and 20%. In other words: **to 'reduce' the relative weight of a section we must extend the others'**.

Conclusions on this grading strategy:

Strengths: 

1. It's very quick to set up. If you like the scales that are predefined or configured by your site administrator (such as: *'Unsatisfactory / Satisfactory / Exceeds expectations'* or *'Present / Absent'*, etc.) you can save a lot of time setting up this section.

2. It is the only one that **allows reviewers to express themselves with numerical grades**. If you want them to grade '7.5', '4', etc. for each other, you can only use this one:

Weaknesses: 

1. My experience with numerical scores is that students get reasons to criticize the subjectivity of the peer-assessment process. Thus comments such as «*what for me is a 'six' for my classmates can be an 'eight and a half'*» can quickly undermine the legitimacy of the workshop. Therefore, **I do not advise forcing them to convert their subjective perceptions into a number**. I prefer to construct written descriptions that are easier to adhere to and that also serve to make explicit those arguments or reasoning on which they are based.

2. Also, the fact that the scales are predefined at the system level –editable by your Moodle administrator– limits the possibilities a lot. If you pull down the menu you'll see that there are just a few available to choose from, and each one offers few intermediate options (usually between two and four) with very little nuance. Later on, when we look at the mathematical background behind the qualification phase, we'll conclude that it's vital to build a wider range of possibilities into these templates.

3. Linguistically we cannot edit them either, so if your course is taught in a language not included among the predefined versions or, worse still, if your subject is precisely about languages you will, of course, prefer to have more control over the section and level designations of the assessment scales.

2. Comments form

We already know that this second evaluation strategy is not really about 'grading', but rather about encouraging cross-feedback among students. Check that, as we move forward, in each *Aspect* we will describe its scope and very little else. These *Aspects* help us to focus their attention and show them what kind of questions evaluators should ask or what kind of elements of the exercise others should learn to detect.

Assessors can then type their observations about each facet of each exercise on screen in that order on an editable **text field**.

By focusing their attention on certain aspects of someone else's exercise, we are indirectly making each of them reflect again on **how they solved their own's**

In case we need to add more aspects

Conclusions on this grading strategy:

Strengths: 

1. Since it is a light type of workshop –this is the only one without the pressure of grading–, it can be useful for teachers **to practice and get used** to its configuration and temporary implementation as well as for students to get used to the format.

2. It is a powerful tool for group dynamics, by establishing the aspects to be discussed.

3. Since the teacher could then **go back to repeat phases** of the workshop, this feedback round can serve very well **as a preliminary round** to propose improvements to the exercises sent and then go back and inform them of the new deadline for submitting exercises to include the suggested improvements. Students can use the feedback they receive to improve their submissions before facing a second, more demanding round. [But watch out, keep reading]

> We will see later, in the '*Allocation*' phase, that if we opt for this option and superimpose another round of co-evaluations it is possible **to mantain the same reviewers-reviewees in the second one**, so that the same students who suggested possible improvements in the first one are the ones who judge in the second one whether they have been taken into account or not

Weaknesses: 

1. If we use a workshop type to do two rounds –first *Comments* and then *Rubric*, for example– those who participate in the first round will receive the plenary (maximum score for both *Submission* and *Assessment*, all, without exception). And if they then do not participate in the second round, **that score will be kept for them**, which would be unfair for the others, who would have complied with the other task, much more demanding. This forces us to manually review the process for fairness, so in the end it is almost preferable to hold two separate workshops.

2. Remember that the other three grading strategies also include the option of a feedback if we enable it in that *Overall feedback mode*, so it turns out that its star functionality is already provided by the others as well.

3. The requested text fields do not allow you to control the number of characters. Therefore, someone could participate in the workshop and complete all these feedback sections with a few short answers, without effort, so that **their laziness would go completely unnoticed** (they would receive the same mark as the others just for having completed the fields) unless we checked it manually afterwards.

3. *Number of errors* form

This grading strategy commands us to define a bunch of *Assertions* to which we want the evaluators to pay attention and judge in an exclusively binary key (*Yes/No, Good/Bad, Compliant/Not Compliant, It is Included/It is not...* etc.). We will freely write both the expression that indicates success and that which implies failure and, again, the relative weight of each aspect if any is more serious or more meritorious than the others.

Workshop: The Great Pyramid of Giza

Number of errors

Assertion 1

Description

Paragraph | B | I

Has he/she analyzed the three main theories?

It only allows **binary** options

Word for the error — No, he/she's forgotten some

Word for the success — Yeah, analyze all three

Weight — 3

Assertion 2

Description

Paragraph | B | I

Has he/she finished with the conclusion as requested?

Word for the error — No

Word for the success — Yes

Weight — 6

▸ Assertion 3

▸ Assertion 4

This is the only grading strategy that allows for **modulating the progressiveness** of the marks (See next pages)

Grade mapping table

Weighted number of errors is less than or equals	Grade for submission
0	100%
6	50%
12	0%

The last section, *Grade mapping table*, forces us –watch!– to adjust the grade according to the number of hits obtained. We will analyze this soon.

Conclusions on this grading strategy:

Strengths: 

1. It is easier for participants to evaluate with this type of concise statements and repetitive format which is so **easy to get used to**.

2. Binary statements *(Success/Error)* are less subjective when correctly worded. This legitimises the evaluation and qualification process of the workshop itself. They also allow the learner to better self-evaluate their own submission and predict what the outcome will be, while forcing them to more consciously **verbalize any mistakes made**.

3. It is the only grading strategy that has that *Grade mapping table* to adjust or rebalance grades . HOWEVER...

Weaknesses: 

1. The configuration of this mapping table is **DANGEROUS**. Please refer to the following two pages before implementing this system 

2. In some cases, it may be more **difficult for teachers to simplify** the aspect evaluated to such an emphatic *yes or no* assertions. Before opting for this type of evaluation, check whether you will indeed be able to compartmentalize all evaluable aspects into binary statements. If you think that some of these aspects require some nuance, remember the rubric also allows you to ask binary questions combined with nuanced questions at different levels.

3. This rating strategy should have been labeled upside down, in positive *–Number of successes–*, since that is how actually the calculations are performed, by adding up the merits, not subtracting them for mistakes. It is precisely the opposite that we miss a lot here. Much could be subtracted for a serious fault (for example an unforgivable spelling mistake) while not making the mistake would not add up to so much, but this possibility does not currently exist.

4. On the other hand, the name of the project is predisposing teachers to foresee and write only the possible **errors** and thus exercises the evaluators in the continuous tracking of the negative aspects of the submissions of others. This is the reason why teachers seem forced to write the opposite or to answer *'Yes'* to *'he made this mistake...'*. To avoid this, it is essential to consciously adopt the opposite perspective and ask for the same aspects in positive (so that the sentence avoids any negation or expression that inverts the statement, as in the example on the previous page). And that the words for the right are also positive, such as *'Yes'*, *'is present'*, *'fulfils'*, etc.). Correcting will be a much more intuitive work for everyone if each exercise evaluated is gaining and **'adding up' little by little as successes are accumulated along the correction grid**, instead of going the opposite way and losing it.

What is that so called *Grade mapping table*?

The *Number of errors* grading strategy deserves a separate explanation for this final section, which makes it unique and very dangerous. Using this *Grading mapping Table,* we must manually modulate the requirement curve, i.e. each percentage of success means obtaining a certain rating. But **if we forget to fill it in and move on to the evaluation phase, all submissions will receive 100% of the grade**. To undo such a mistake we would have to *delete* all the evaluations and advise the participants to fill in the evaluation headings again. This is the last thing we would want to happen. So let's see how it works:

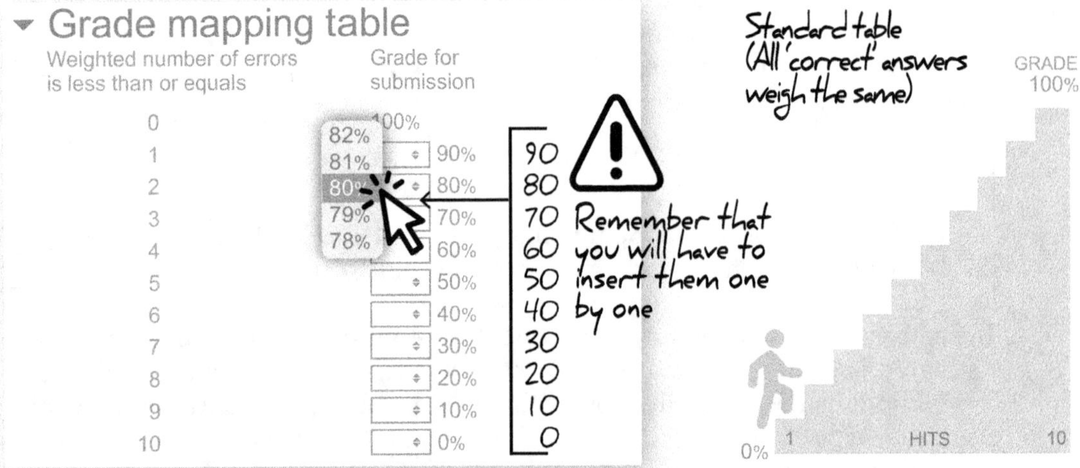

If we insert the values as indicated by default, all the hits would add up to the same.

Now let's say that because of the high demands of the exercise we are asking for, we decided that **a couple of mistakes could be forgiven**. So any one or two mistakes are perfectly acceptable with a *Full mark*, instead of the 80% that would correspond to the eight correct answers. In that case we will manually remap the grade assigned to those 2 mistakes and increase your grade up to, for example, 96%. From this, we will **calculate proportionally the other grades** (for example, four correct answers would become almost a 'pass', and on the opposite side we would set 98% for nine corrects).

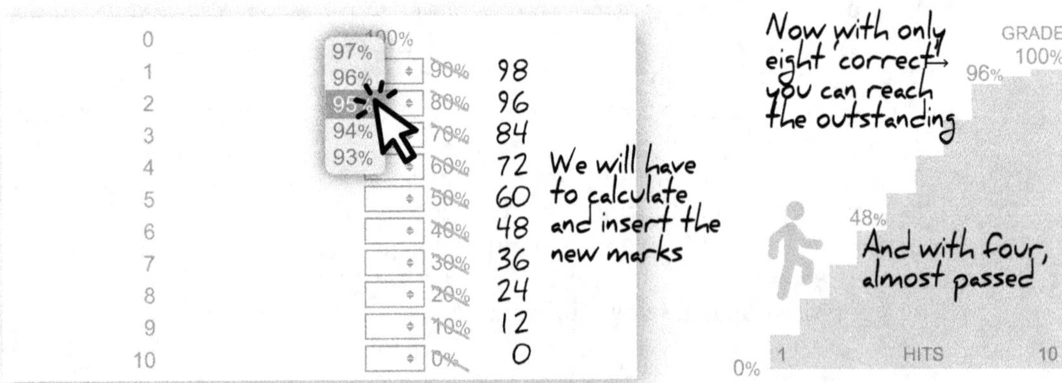

Or the other way around. The opposite may be the case: that we need to reduce the merit of the hits. On one occasion, an assistant at the *Teach Twice course* asked his pupils to write an exercise and he wanted to design a rubric that would prevent possible spelling mistakes in the following way: that committing a serious fault –such as confusing a B letter for a V, forgetting an H, etc.– would substract a lot, but, on the other hand, typing correctly would not add up to so many points, of course. Otherwise, by the fact of writing normally one could get a high mark. For a case like this, this *Grade mapping table* would allow us to compress the grades from below by configuring a first bar in, for example, seven hits, which could be required to pass (50%) and the last three to reach the maximum grade. Note how in this case the first hits have almost lost their merit (we need many to get a pass) and *viceversa*, those first three errors subtract a lot from the grade.

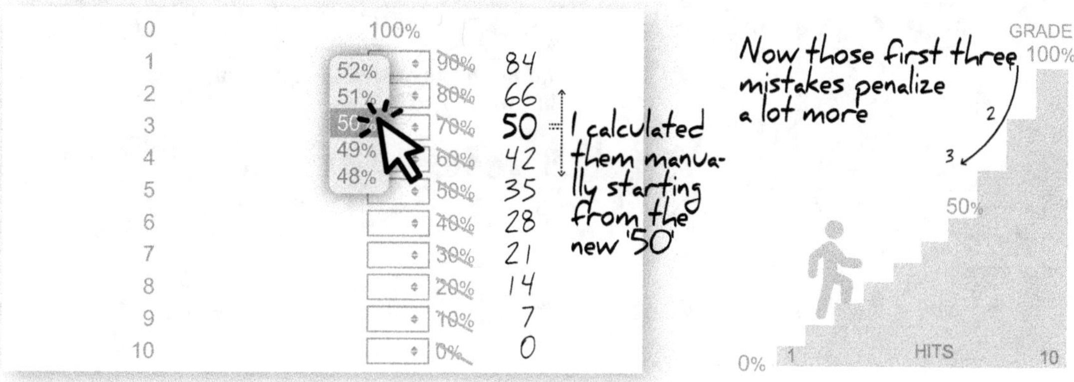

In the first column they are shown as *Weighted number of errors is less than or equal* to the maximum that can be committed. Thus, if we have left three statements defined, one with a value of '4', another with a value of '7' and the last of '2', the total number of errors that could be made would be 13. Note that although a student could only obtain scores that are a multiple of these three figures (i.e. in this case only these eight combinations: 0, 2, 4, 6, 7, 9, 11 and 13) the column provides all the intermediate scores as well. And the indicative score for each section, in percentages without decimals.

Remember that here we are not directly awarding 'points' to the student, **but rather a percentage on that grade** for the submission that we left configured in the workshop *Settings*

Be careful here. Again if we include a new statement or delete another one, because after any change we will have to **complete again in full all the values** of the mapping table so that this last change is taken into account. This is so annoying.

A quick way to decide these stretches is to **establish the new 'pass' mark**. That is to say, to choose the intermediate point that adapts more to what we need (for example if I want to hinder the pass, I think: «*Of the total 14 possible successes, it will be allowed to fail not the half, but only five to pass*») and then adjust this new percentage with the drop-down menu to 'five mistakes', assigning that 50% of the grade. We will then distribute the first five points among the first nine correct hits (5.5% each), rounding up the decimals, and the last five points thereafter, with the remaining five correct hits (10% each). The graphic above shows visually the new proportions.

4. *Rubric* form

It is the most versatile rating strategy. It allows us to define as many evaluation criteria as we wish so that they can be evaluated in any of the other three ways seen so far
(since here we can freely write scales with the levels of correction we want to establish
-'*Bad/Regular/Good/Excellent*'–, or binary statements '*Yes/No*'). To these criteria we
can also freely assign their respective numerical values or request comments.

Workshop: The Great Pyramid of Giza

Rubric

▾ Criterion 1
Description

Párrafo   B *I*

Did he/she answered the question that was asked?

They will always end up showing in order, from least to most

Level grade and definition | 0 | No. It's gone off the rails
Level grade and definition | 6 | Yes, although not in depth
Level grade and definition | 10 | Yes, satisfactorily

▾ Criterion 2
Description

Paragraph   B *I*

Did he/she put in relation the content of the documentary to the three theories explained in the classroom?

If you need to add more levels, fill in the last one and press 'save and continue editing'

Level grade and definition | 0 | No, not to any
Level grade and definition | 4 | Yes, to one
Level grade and definition | 7 | Yes, to two
Level grade and definition | 9 | Yes, to al three

▾ Criterion 3
Description

Paragraph   B *I*

Was the requested page length limit respected?

Students will not see these numerical values, but only the definitions

Level grade and definition | 0 | No
Level grade and definition | 5 | Sí

There are a couple of technical limitations to be taken into account when drafting rubrics:

Firstly, regardless of the order in which we write the definitions, once the grade has been assigned to each level they **will be shown on the screen according to that score**. That is, if we assign three levels to *Criterion 1* –which we have described as «*Level of Originality*»– «*High / Low / Regular*» with their respective values 10 / 0 / 5, Moodle will automatically reorder them so that they are read on screen from less to more, that is: «*Low / Regular / High*». This is not a problem for short descriptions, but it can be a serious obstacle when writing descriptions with more elaborate or interdependent sentences and interlaced wording. So, keeping this in mind, let's be careful when constructing our self-explanatory rubrics, always starting from the 'worst' to the 'best'.

Secondly, all the levels of the same criterion must have **different numerical values** (it would not be possible to repeat, for example: 0/5/5/10).

Finally, the option *Save and Preview* will allow us to look at the final result on screen before giving the approval. There are two display options: **List** and **Grid**. Depending on the length of the statements and the complexity of your categories, one or the other will be more appropriate. Always think about the adaptability/responsiveness to your users' devices. Although we work on a computer monitor more and more our students will visualize that rubric from their respective smartphones and tablets and will click not with the mouse but with their own fingers.

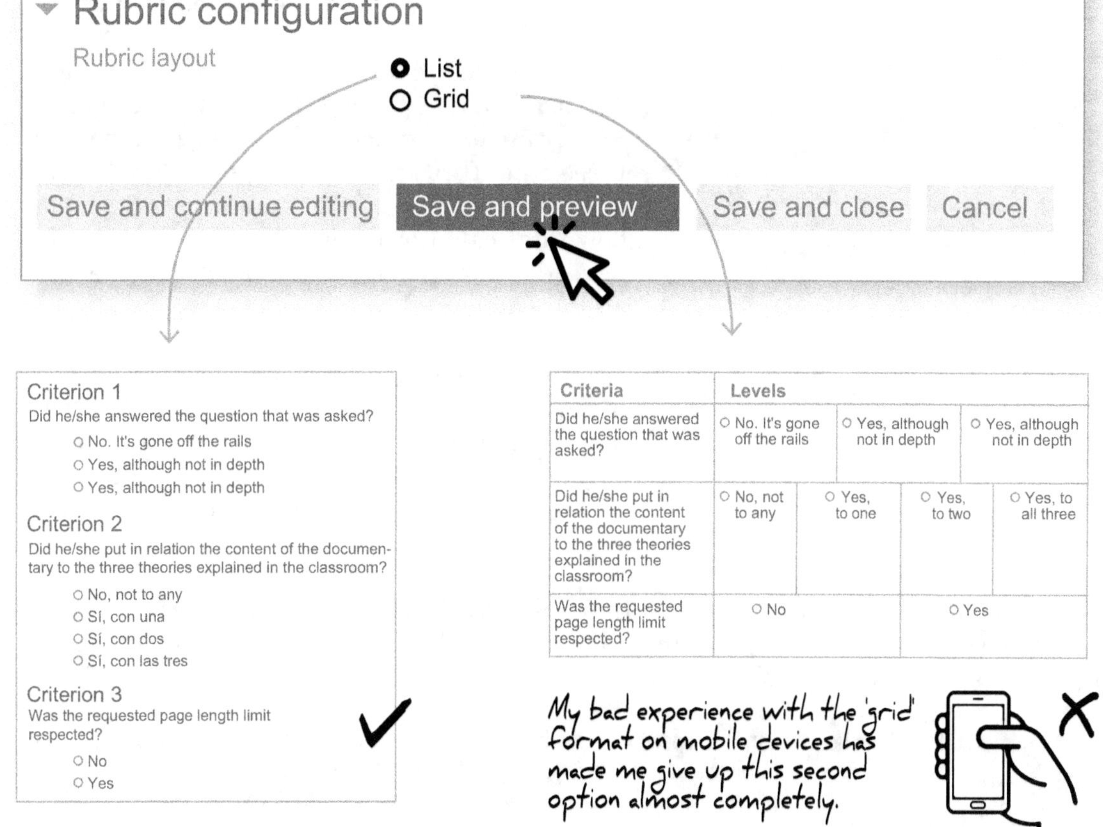

My bad experience with the 'grid' format on mobile devices has made me give up this second option almost completely.

If you're going to need more numerical nuance, take advantage of the drop-down menu to play with higher values, each from zero to one hundred. So, if you were planning to give a scale with these four values: 0/1/1/2 where the two central ones were the same, you can take advantage of the full range of the drop-down menu and replace them with 0/49/50/100, which has a mathematically similar function.

However, in this case, when computing the assessors' score (judging the adjudicator) it will also be the case that Moodle will consider them to be almost the same answer, i.e. as there is almost no quantitative difference between the second option (49 points) and the third option (50) it will consider one or the other answer practically equivalent and **will discriminate very little**.

Perhaps you missed each criterion its respective **Weighting** that was previously present in the *Aspects* and the *Assertions* respectively. In the case of the *Rubric* it does not appear. It is unnecessary, since as here we are freely defining those minimum, intermediate and maximum values –each from zero to one-hundred–, by doing so we are already directly setting their weight. Thus, if, for example, we wanted to assign a normal value to the first criterion (divided into four levels, for example: 0/1/2/3) and we believe that the second criterion should weigh three times as much, it would be sufficient to increase the value of its levels proportionally (0/3/6/9) and so on with the rest of the criteria.

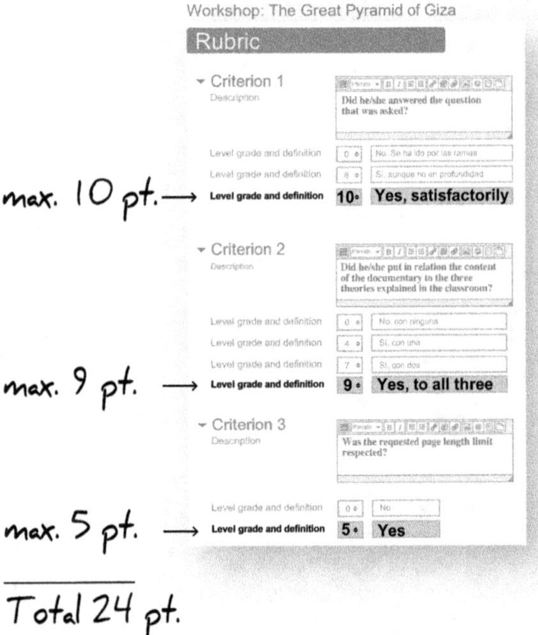

The system considers that the total value of each criterion is **the maximum score that can be obtained on it**. In the illustrated example there would be 10, 9 and 5 respectively, so we would already have accumulated a maximum of 24.

Let us say that to finish off this rubric we would like to add a fourth and final criterion, the most important one, which will weigh as much as these other three together. Then we should give it a maximum value of 24 and from there build down its scale (for example, if we wanted it to have four levels it could be: 0/9/17/24) so the new accumulated total would be 48.

Let's remember that **we are not assigning 'points' directly to each section**, but only balancing their respective relative weights. That's why we don't care so much about how much they add up to in total, but only about their relative proportions.

As we know, the points that were worth both the *Submission* and the *Assessment* **are already set** in the workshop *Settings*, at the *Grade Settings* section. We should come back there if we want to change them.

On the internet you can find repositories of rubrics that have been used and shared by other teachers, especially for summative evaluation. The Association of Universities and Institutes offers a select battery of 16 multidisciplinary rubrics **https://www.aacu.org/value-rubrics**. If you are building it for the first time, it is highly advisable to check its wording first to get inspiration from these examples

Conclusions on this grading strategy:

Strengths: 

1. Although with its own limitations, the *Rubric* is by far the most **versatile, flexible and adaptable** of the four grading strategies. It allows you to build rating tables similar to those offered by *Acumulative Grading* and *Number of Errors*, which is not possible the other way around.

2. It allows a finer finish and greater control of the final visual appearance that our answer grid will have on screen, as well as modulating and freely subdividing the numerical values of each level.

3. One could say that the *Rubric* **unfolds all the potentialities of the peer assessment** workshop, which almost seems to be built around this concept.

Weaknesses: 

1. It is indeed because of that versatility and potential that **forces us teachers to build it more carefully** –which makes it almost essential to have it prepared beforehand–. It requires a greater degree of intellectual effort.

2. It does not allow for reordering criteria once they have been constructed. So if after finishing it you decide to include a new one or change the order of the criteria, you will have to move one by one the contents of the boxes to their new positions. The process of modification can be so tedious, slow and risky that I advise to **redo from scratch all the fields we want to modify**. This is one more reason why it is almost essential to build the rubric separately, in another document get our calculations prepared outside the web and then proceed to translate it quietly on the platform.

How to adapt my rubrics **to Moodle**

Remember to always include the value 'ZERO' that Moodle needs as the basis of the scale

Criterion 1

Answering the question. (15 pts.)

15   Yes, satisfactorily
8   Yes, although not in depth
0 No. It's gone off the rails

Criterion 2

Does he/she relate the content of the to the two theories explained in the classroom?

~~10~~   Good
~~0~~   Bad
~~5~~   Regular

Write them in order from least to most, as your students will read them

0 Bad
5 Regular
10 Good

Always provide for the possibility of 'blank/in-valid answer' otherwise a half-baked exercise would get 5 points here

Criterion 3

Exceeds word limit:

0   **Submission not valid**
1   Yes
5   No

"NOTE: "Falling short in meeting two of the three criteria will result in direct failure"

The criteria cannot be interrelated/multiplied/divi-ded. Everything adds up or doesn't. Nothing else

How to write them more **efficiently**

Avoid verbs in the present tense, preferably in the past tense, and questions: Has he/she answered... Did the answer include....?

Criterion 1

~~Answering~~ the question. (15 pts.)
¿Did he/she answer...

0   No. It's gone off the rails
7   Yes, although not in depth
15   Yes, satisfactorily

Do never mention the grades. On the contrary, the one being assessed is THE REVIEWER him/herself, who now must act and answer correctly

Criterion 2

Does he/she relate the content of the to the two theories explained in the classroom?

0   ~~Bad~~   **Worse than average**
5   ~~Regular~~   **On the average**
10   ~~Good~~   **It stands out from the other exercises**

Let's avoid adjectives. If it is still necessary to make value judgments, one way of objectifying them is to consider the rest as standards

Criterion 3

Does it ~~violate~~ the word limit?
       ...meet..

0   ~~Yes~~   **Exceeded the maximum limit**
5   ~~No~~   **Respected the maximum limit**

Write in positive (Has he gone? ...has he fulfilled? ...) Always ask for the successes, not for the mistakes

Submission

Teachers:

We'll just sit here and watch. As the early bird students are delivering, we will take the opportunity to **open those first exercises and snoop around. This is very convenient** since we will have surprises that will make us rethink the rubric or even rectify instructions

Students:

At this stage they can finally submit their exercises (unless we set a different deadline under 'Adjustments', beware)

2. Submission phase

This is the stage for **receiving** the exercises and the first time the students have access to the workshop. Finally, they become the real protagonists.

The workshop never enters this submission phase by itself. Only when we manually click on Switch to the next phase –or on the corresponding black circle on their icon– the students will be able to start uploading their assignments. Until now, the workshop only showed them a laconic «*The workshop is being configured*» that allowed them to know its *Title*, *Description* and location in the course, but nothing else. They were not able to submit or read any instructions yet.

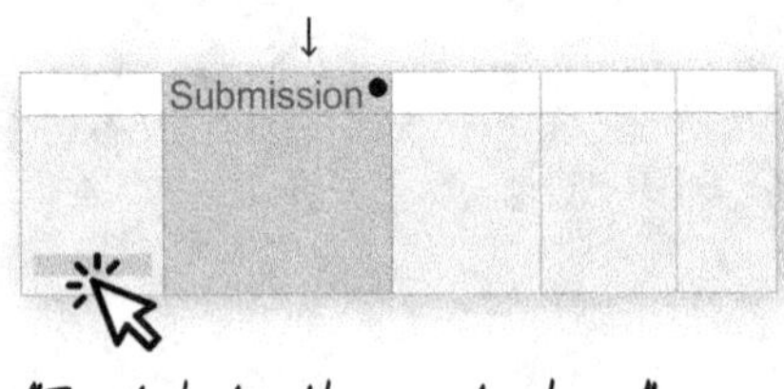

"Switch to the next phase"

Now, while the students can see the instructions and are finally able to participate in the activity, the teacher can **continue configuring the rest of the sections of the workshop –especially the rubric– and at the same time can take a look at the first submissions**. It is very important to review those first exercises as they arrive because if there had been any mismatch –and there are plenty of occasions for that to happen– we would still be in time to stop the process, fix it and warn the participants of the change or potential misunderstandings.

Remember that if you had enabled the time restriction in 'Settings' and that deadline had not yet been met, **it would be impossible for them to submit their work**. It's not enough to have passed manually to this phase, but that other condition must also be fulfilled so that finally the activity is opened at the reception of the exercises.

What they see:

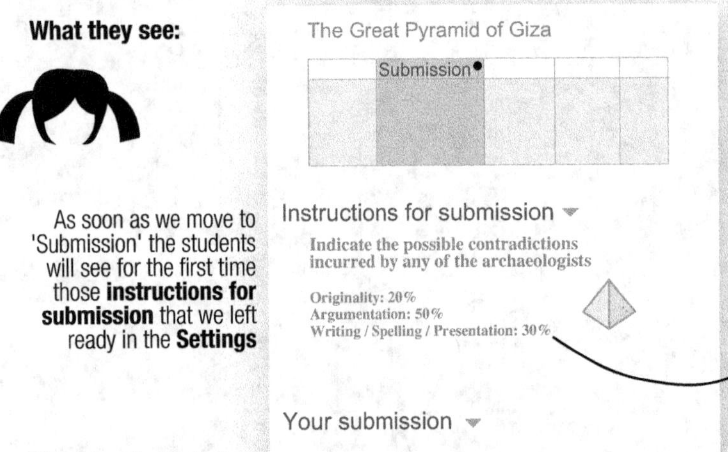

As soon as we move to 'Submission' the students will see for the first time those **instructions for submission** that we left ready in the **Settings**

The upload button invites them to **"Start"** to prepare your submission

Remember the importance of having anticipated, if only briefly, what the valuation criteria will be

Let's remember that we teachers usually work on Moodle in a self-absorbed way and usually without supervision from others. When students observe some kind of anomaly, each one of them will react differently.

For example, let's say that in the statement we explicitly ask them to submit the assignment in a PDF file and we forgot to check the corresponding box in that *Submission types / File attachment.* It will happen that some participants will wait, passively, without delivering until the problem is solved by itself. Others, more intrepid, will copy their finished text, extract it from the file and paste it into the submission window in order to proceed... Finally, by the time one of them takes the initiative to inform us of the problem, the casuistry of each exercise submitted will already be so extensive that it will be impossible for us to continue with the next phase (evaluation by rubric) in a minimally fair way because the evaluators will give disparate marks. When faced with the same exercise, some will click on *Not satisfactory* and others on *Satisfactory* with the same good intentions if they do not know that there were these previous problems.

Sometimes it can happen that although we believe that everything is correctly configured and the students have received (and understood) the necessary information to participate, in reality there are so many circumstances that can lead to misinterpretations, broken links, screens of different sizes that show one content or another... That is why it is vital to **check diligently whether these first submissions meet our expectations**.

But the most important reason to look at these first answers is that they are an inexhaustible source of information to improve our evaluation form. Remember that during this phase your rubric is not yet published or the possible errors to look at, the aspects to comment on, etc. Even if you think you have foreseen all the possible misconceptions/errors/merits or elements judged by your peers, students will always surprise you. The casuistry of implausible deviations that each of them is capable of exploring is impossible for the teacher to foresee.

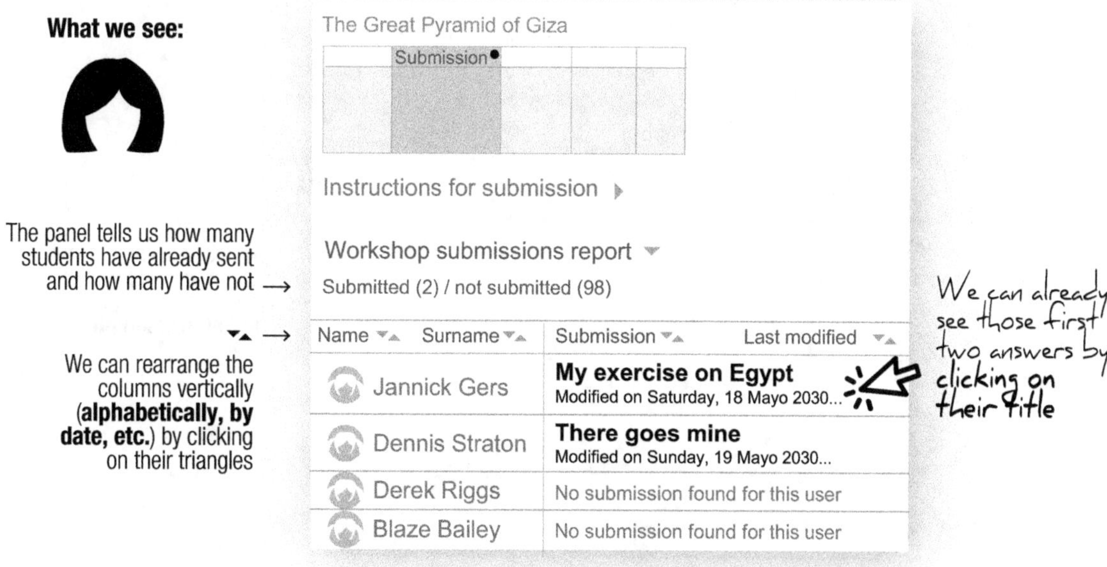

Although I have set up dozens of workshops to date, it has not yet been the case that I have **not had to readjust my rubric** in light of my students' first submissions. Course after course and even if I repeat exactly the same instructions the refinement task seems to be infinite.

And somehow it is also the workshop itself that benefits and is refined by its own use. The fact that the rubric and its evaluation criteria can be modified and improved during this *Phase 2* is vital for the whole activity to move towards the ideal of formative and fair evaluation. But, of course, that patch needs to be done now, before we move on to allocating reviews (*Phase 3*) or they start applying the rubric (*Phase 4*).

Can they modify or delete their exercise once it has been submitted?

Yes, during the *Submission* phase participants can upload another exercise or delete the one they submitted. Unlike the other Moodle tasks, where we can avoid 'reopening' –so if a student regrets their answer they can no longer go back– in the workshops they can do so whenever, as long as we are still in this phase. As well as *Delete* their work, while it has not yet been peer-assessed.

This text is the only confirmation they see that their exercise has indeed been delivered. It often happens that **they are not aware of** it, which creates uncertainty

Each student can change their answer, delete it or upload a new one **during the Submission phase**

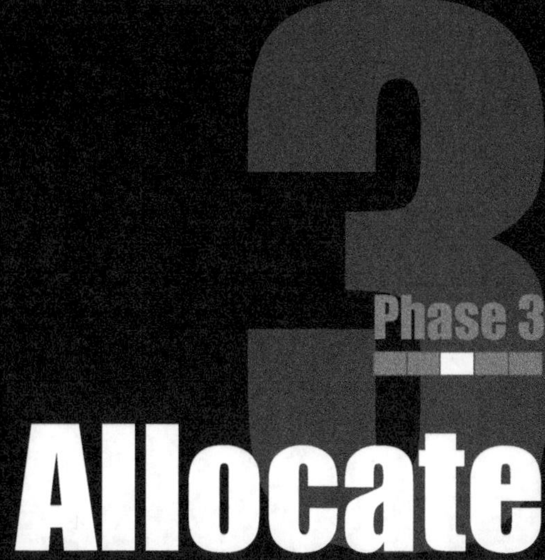

Allocate

Teachers:

This phase is devoted to assign each student the number of exercises they must asses. It may only take a second (one click, if the default options work for you) **and thus avoid this entire chapter.** But if you want to investigate thoroughly how it works, you will discover its enormous potential

Students:

Once the Submission phase is finished, the **students stay waiting for us to assign** them exercises in order to proceed with the next one, the Assessment phase

3. Allocate submissions

Although Moodle doesn't seem to give it the status of a distinct 'phase' or a column with its own heading at this point, the allocation of tasks that each participant is going to review should deserve a separate section. This is one of the most interesting moments of the workshop. You can access it like this:

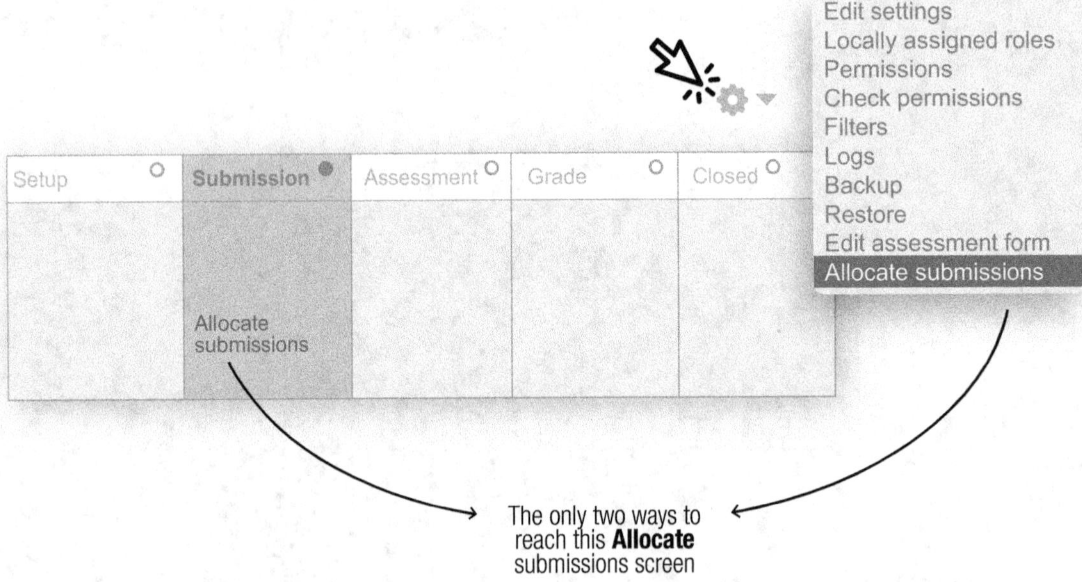

The only two ways to reach this **Allocate** submissions screen

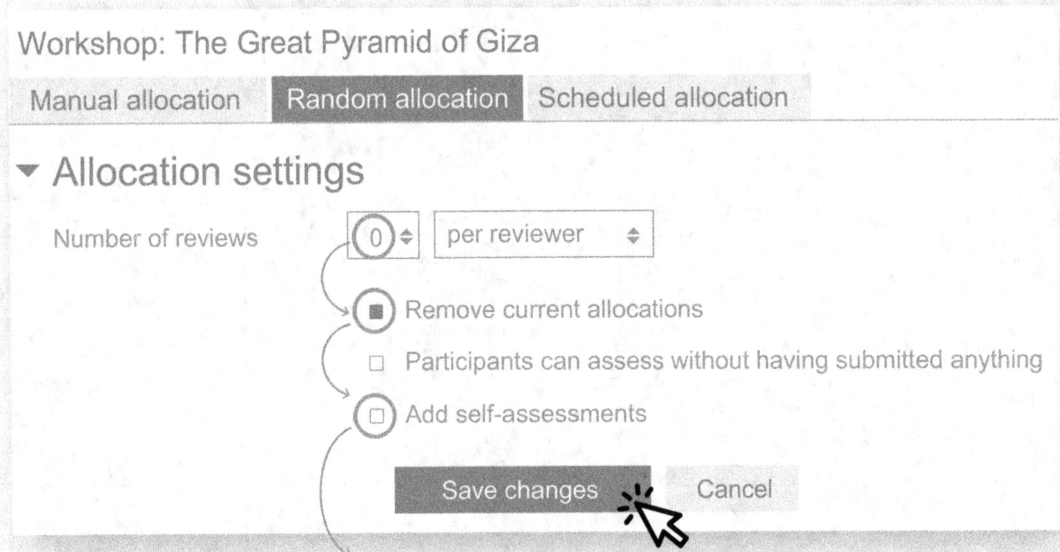

To reset allocations: choose 'zero' evaluations, activate 'remove' the current ones and disable the self-assessments

Before you proceed with it, keep in mind that...

1. To begin the assignment we need the students **to have already finished handing in** their homework. There would be several ways to cut that exercise input. For example: go back momentarily to the previous phase –the *Setup* phase, in which no submissions can be made– or leave the time limit we saw (*Date* and *Time*) from the *Settings* set in advance. It would also be possible to cut off this flow by going to the next phase –*Assessment*– but in this case the reviewers would find this contradiction on the screen: The workshop is already ready to start evaluating and yet no exercises are assigned. So let's avoid this third option. If you wish, you can also momentarily 'hide' the workshop from the course page.

> If under Settings you enabled the option *«Change to the next phase after the deadline for submissions»* this advance to *Assessment'* the change could have already happened automatically. Beware

2. This moment of the allocation of submissions is a **private** phase, only visible to the teacher. We can make mistakes, make tests, reassign, etc. as many times as we need, since students will only see these assignments when we click on *Switch to the next phase*, the *Assessment* one, which will be, yes, public.

> In fact, **you can delete all the allocations you are trying to make at any time**. (See illustration on previous page) Simply select 'Zero' evaluations, as well as *«Remove current allocations»* and deactivate *«Add self-assessments»*. Saving changes will reset all assignments. You can therefore try out all the possibilities without fear of combining them, rectify and familiarise yourself with this menu as long as you do not advance the workshop to the next phase: *Assessment*. On the other hand, if you are deleting them later, when students have already assessed each other, this general deletion **would respect those assessments. Only assignments that have not yet been peer reviewed could be therefore deleted**.

3. One of the most peculiar characteristics of this assignment of evaluators –that each student can also self-review their own work– is configured in this menu, but only if –remember– we had left it activated before, in the main workshop *Settings*. We will need to go back there if we forgot to activate it.

4. Another of the workshop's pedagogically more interesting features is the option that even the participants **who did not submit** their exercise –and therefore missed that chance to get the first part of the grade– can now re-engage in the workshop and have a second chance to learn and exercise during this other phase, now reviewing the others' answers and achieving at least that other half of the grade. This is one of the strengths of the workshop.

5. Finally, that if we enable the option *Allow submissions after the deadline*, we should be attentive to the stragglers and remember later to assign specifically to them both submissions to evaluate and evaluators to review theirs'.

And how many tasks should I assign to each reviewer?

Well, the answer is clear: **more than you thought**. Let's see why.

We are free to choose the number of submissions to be assigned to each participant for evaluation: from only one to up to thirty (or the number of participants in the task. Between 0 and 10 the number is free, from then on only 15, 20 and 30 are allowed). And since Moodle will calculate the grade of each submission **by doing the arithmetic average of those received**, the more evaluations a given exercise receives the closer it will come to its objectively deserved grade and the harder it will be for a malicious or uninformed participant to over-influence it.

> Although at first sight it may seem to us that four or five evaluations are enough and we are already 'exploiting them too much' in this work that usually would be the responsibility of the teachers, in practice you will see –if you observe them while they carry it out– that **the application of a good rubric is a much quicker task than it seems**. I advise you to spend much more time designing it well so that you will then have no problem requiring them to evaluate a larger number of participants (for example, seven, nine, fifteen...)

But, even more decisive: the grade that the judges themselves will receive as reviewers is based on what each one has moved away from the consensus (the average), so that below three evaluators (with two) there is no difference in terms of dissent (both move equally away from the average) and automatically both get a 'full' mark. So consider **3 as the minimum number of judges acceptable**.

> We will comment later on that it is usually more convenient to use **odd** numbers. Personally, I recommend a minimum of **seven or nine** evaluations per submission, depending on the volume of work to be evaluated.

Remember also that even if you assign them submissions to evaluate this does not guarantee that they will all comply with this second part of the exercise. Moreover, if you consider giving the stragglers entry in this new phase of Evaluation –activating that option «*Participants can assess without having submitted anything*»– it is very possible that the participation rate will be reduced even more. From my experience: don't be surprised if almost all those students who missed the first opportunity also gave up this second one that you were offering them with all your good will.

Better to allocate per submission or per reviewer?   `7 ⇕` `per reviewer ⇕` `✓ per reviewer` `per submission`

Per reviewer. No doubt, since it gives you more control over the final outcome. This way, all participants have the same workload and more allocations are obtained than *Per submission*, for the simple reason that the number of reviewers (participants) will always be higher than the number of submissions –and, moreover, predictable in advance–.

Once you have taken all this into account, you can try out the allocation system you need from among these three types, each one indicated in one of the upper tabs:

> *Manual*: You choose one by one who evaluates whom
> *Random*: Moodle pairs them randomly
> *Scheduled*: Also at random but with the possibility of planning it in advance so that the system can do it later automatically, at the end of the submission phase.

Random Allocation:

The first time we allocate submissions, it's a good idea to start with the *Random* one. The settings for this assignment mode are very intuitive:

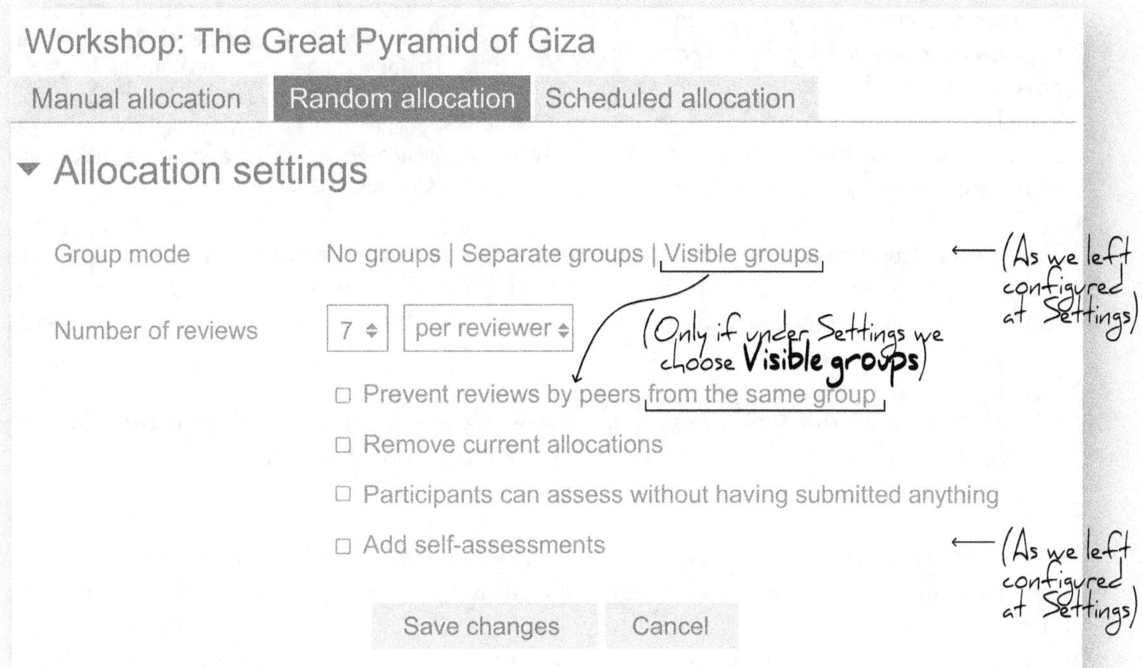

The ***Group mode*** informs us of what we choose in the *Settings*: The mixing of *all with all* (there are *No groups* / *'totum revolutum'*, so that anyone can also review any other) or, conversely, if each student can only be evaluated by members of the same group (*'Separate groups'*), which works in practice as several mini workshops of watertight peer-assessment). In this case, each participant would only see, evaluate and be evaluated by the others in his or her group.

But of course, for this it is necessary that these groups exist previously and to have left it enabled previously in the *Settings* section as we saw.

This case of peer-evaluation **within the group** is very common: let's say that your students have submitted an essay completed among several and then you would like to ask them who has worked harder than the others or in what aspect each one has shone. If you have those same groups ordered and perfectly classified in Moodle (remember the installable '**Group Autoselect**' plug-in [Page 31], so that the students themselves are organized in groups instead of us having to do this tedious work) you can now comfortably assign those peer-evaluations. However, if the groups are small (for example, four components, where each one is only evaluated by three others) remember that the *Grade for submission* will have important deviations, so only the other one, the *Grade for assessment*, would be significant. Therefore, if it is a manageable class, consider whether you can no longer settle it by passing a paper form/questionnaire and manually doing the sums.

But on this screen the *Group mode* section is actually working as a **mere reminder** of the decision we already made before. To change the selection we would need to go back to *Settings*.

Special mention should be made of the third option, entitled *Visible Groups,* because it introduces the very interesting opposite option: «*Prevent reviews by peers from the same group*». That is, instead of reducing the scope of work to one's own group, this option, on the contrary, only excludes the members of each group from evaluating each other.

Let's say, for example, that my students have prepared an oral presentation in the classroom in groups of four. Then I want them to evaluate **how they felt about other student's presentations**. If I have the same groups created in Moodle, I can set up the workshop with 'visible groups' and then, by activating this option, prevent everyone from evaluating the presentation they participated in.

If in any of these cases you had **a student off the hook**, outside of any group, the system itself would alert you that: «*...users MUST BE members of at least one group in order to have peer review...*» and adds another warning below with the specific list of students who would be out of the draw.

The next option, '*Number of reviews*', invites us to select the number of submissions that will be assigned to each of the participants or, conversely, the number of participants that should review each submission.

Notice how the 'number' of assignments drop-down list includes the option '**zero**', apparently useless, but which, on the contrary, allows us to do something very important: delete all the assignments so that, for example, we can **reset and repeat** the process again as many times as we need. To do this, it would be enough to combine it with *Remove current allocations.*

Regarding '*Remove current allocations*'. This reassuring section reminds us that only if we want to, the changes we are introducing will modify the already established pairings. So, we can continue testing, as the new allocations will only be added to the existing ones. And when we want to make a clean slate and establish new pairings from scratch, we only need to activate it together with '**0 per reviewer**'.

The consequence of this very important option is that we could continue to generate random allocations even **with the assessment phase already underway** or even after a closed or qualified workshop has been reopened. In other words, Moodle is giving us the peace of mind that all this work that affects so many people (there may already be students evaluating colleagues or we may even have finished grading the whole workshop) is safe and we can continue to set up new assignments that will only overlap the previous allocations, without stepping or deleting them if we don't want.

What if my students have already started to evaluate each other and I return to this assignment screen...? Could I accidentally delete that work, those evaluations already completed by them, if I delete allocations? Happily the answer is 'no'. After reviewing other people's work in the next phase, those grades for both the submission and the respective **reviewers are saved**. It is possible to manually delete them one by one from the control panel if you wish, but you can be sure that there is no danger of mistakenly deleting evaluations that have already been made, no matter how much you play with this *Allocation* section. The pairings that we could delete would be those that have not yet been completed, i.e. that have not yet set up in an assessment (and which you will see will be shown temporarily in red), but we will not accidentally lose those advances made by the students.

Finally, the implications of the last two options have already been discussed above. Remember that «***Participants can evaluate without having sent anything***» is a very good option to reengage the laggards in the activity but **it will greatly reduce the percentage of participation in the next phase**, since it is very possible that they will also fail this other half of the task

Therefore, if you want to guarantee, for example, 7 evaluations for each exercise, you should consider starting from a higher number (for example, 10), since perhaps thirty percent of the participants will not comply with it. From my experience, that is the proportion of students who fail to complete the optional exercises we do during the course. But keep reading, as below I explain there is a much better and more elaborate solution that I discovered only through practice.

My advice if you're going to mix up participants who fulfilled their task by submitting their work with others who didn't:

If, in this draw of random assignments, both predictably compliant students (the punctual ones, who have already submitted their work and seem to keep acting responsibly) and those more lazy ones (who have not submitted their work, so it is quite possible that they will not complete this second phase either), what will happen is this: As a result of chance, some exercises will have more compliant students –and therefore more completed assessments and a more 'fair' grade– and others less –and therefore, with the opposite effect–. Personally, I tried to fight against this unpredictable circumstance by adding more revision work (instead of, for example, 7 assignments, going up to 10) to mitigate this effect of chance, until I realized that I could solve it in another way, by means of **a two-step allocation**:

First, I make a random assignment of **7** reviewers **per submission** exclusively among the submitters (by unchecking the box «*Participants can evaluate without having sent anything*»). In this way I maximize the chances that each and every submitted paper can be reviewed by seven compliant peers.

And then I make a second random assignment including also the students who did not submit anything (check the box) in this case of **7** reviews **per reviewer** respecting the previous assignments (unchecked «*Remove current allocations*»).

When you click on *Save changes* the system will be forced to assign seven assignments to each of these students who did not enter the first draw, so their assignments will be **an addition to the other seven** that each exercise already had.

If you test this you will see that the final result is that all the participants have an equal workload (they all have 7 assignments to evaluate) but each exercise will have a variable number of evaluators –and this is not so worrying– made up of seven 'compliant' jurors and, in addition, some of these other students, newcomers, who will probably not even evaluate.

Finally, with respect to ***Add self-assessments***; if we activate it, the system will assign each participant who submits his or her assignment one more paper in addition to those seven, his or her own, to be evaluated as the eighth. In fact, it will **appear in last place**. And for those who did not submit, it will not.

For example, if you were thinking of setting up the workshop **exclusively as a self-assessment exercise**, indicate 'ZERO' assignments per reviewer and then activate the self-assessment. As a result, everyone will receive theirs exclusively.

Lastly, all the specifications indicated will display their effects when we click on ***Save Changes***. After a few seconds, the crosses will be shown on the screen on a green background, which will only include the exercises that were already sent and the users that are computable at that time.

What about that single exercise that is usually delivered out of time?

Any new submission that we accept —that is, a participant that joins from this moment on— **will be momentarily unassigned**, without being able to participate neither actively nor passively in the *Assessment* phase, as long as we do not repeat any of these allocation processes to include them in the draw.

Let's say that a student has arrived late and we accept their submission in the middle of the evaluation phase, when many of the other classmates already have their reviews assigned and are immersed in that task (for example, they all evaluate seven and *viceversa*, all the assignments are already evaluated by seven people). Now who evaluates the newcomer? If in *Number of reviews* we choose again 7 *per submission* and click on *Save changes*, this last exercise will be assigned to seven other people to review —who will now see their load slightly increased with respect to the rest, since these seven people will have to evaluate one more assignment, the eighth, and maybe we should even notify them personally, because they thought they had already fulfilled their obligation and perhaps they have put this issue aside, they have disengaged from the activity that they rightly thought was over—.

But, besides that, the tardy student will not yet have signed submissions to review. We will have to select again in *Number of reviews* 7 but in this case *per reviewer*, so that, now yes, the straggler student is assigned his task. In this way he will be able to evaluate seven other classmates —as the eighth evaluator of each of them— something that no longer worries us so much but, on the contrary, will add more reliability to those results.

Let's also say that if we wish, we can **later manually adjust** all these assignments that will be generated here automatically by switching to *Manual* mode whenever we wish.

Scheduled allocation:

This type of allocation is a copy of the previous one and in fact all the comments we have made so far are useful here –it is also 'random'– but with the only and great difference of being the only one that does allow to postpone that moment of the assignment. It replicates in all its aspects the random assignment but leaving that final click of the *Save changes* button planned for another time. What time? The one we enabled in *Settings* as the limit for deliveries. In fact, if we have forgotten to do so, the system will kindly inform us that «*Unable to automatically allocate submissions* [since] *Workshop does not have the submissions deadline defined*».

Workshop: The Great Pyramid of Giza

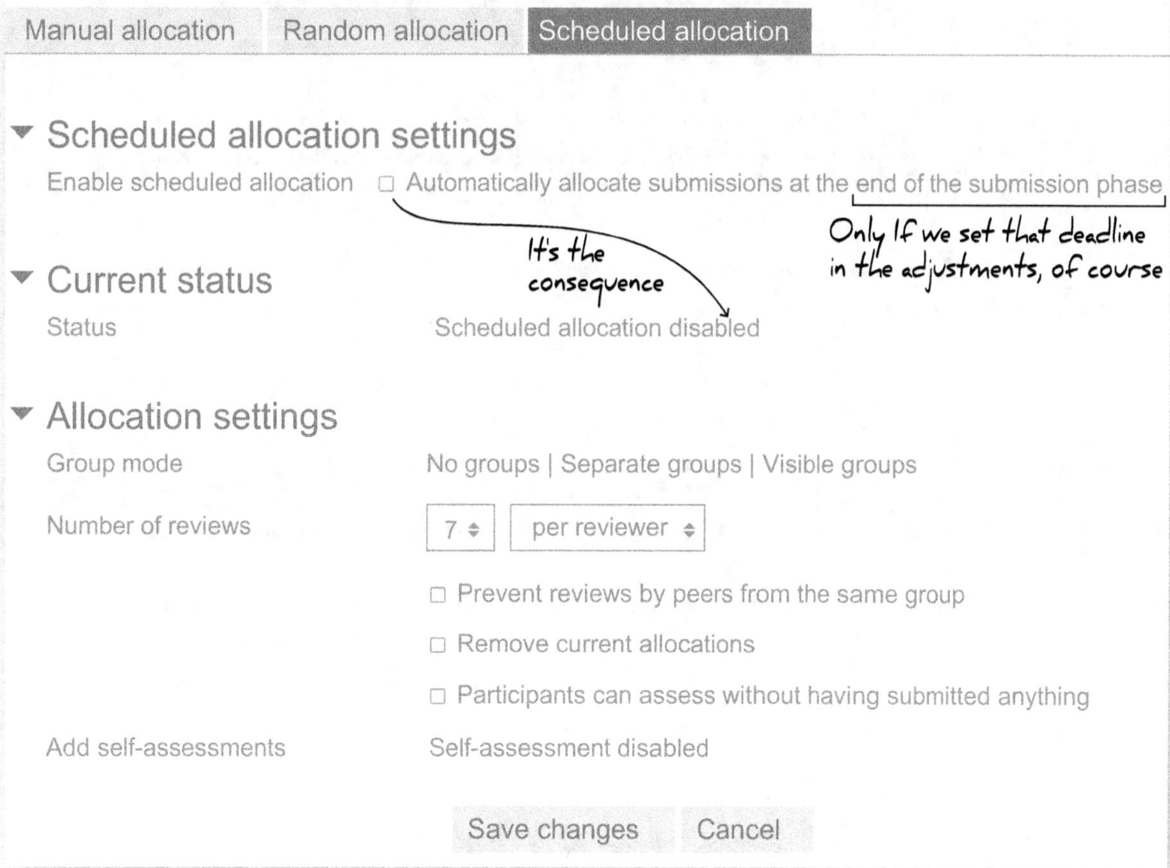

We know that in *Settings* we could also leave the automatic jump from the *Submission* to the *Assessment* phase programmed by means of that button entitled «*Switch to the next phase after the submissions deadline*». Well, if we leave this type of scheduled assignment planned in addition to the change of phase, the students will be able to continue with the activity without us having to do anything here.

In summary, the necessary adjustments for the workshop to advance **automatically** through these intermediate phases would be as follows:

How to automate the transition between phases

In 'Setting's, under the section '**Availability**':

1. We enable a date and time for the start of reception of submissions, but more importantly, a time limit as deadline to those submissions

2. Just with the following button «Switch to the next phase after the submissions deadline» we activate this automatic transition

3. Below, we disable the deadline for starting assessments (date/time)

In this way, the deadline for submissions works automatically as the start of the evaluation phase. Optionally, you could also impose the closing deadline of this second phase here.

Then, from the Control Panel, under '**Allocate Submissions**'

4. We enable the scheduled assignment with the button «Automatically allocate submissions at the end of the submission phase», and also there, the rest of the settings that we could prefer.

5. Press 'Save changes' and wait for the platform to confirm that the Scheduled allocation has been enabled.

Manual allocation

Why have we left this allocation mode until the end, when its tab appears in first position? At first glance it seems to be intended for small or more manageable groups, where the teacher is able to design the pairings to his or her liking. However, in practice it is more useful as a **complement to the other two modes**; random and scheduled, to make fine adjustments.

The interface is intuitive. In the central column we see named the participants and in each of the two sides, respectively, by whom they're reviewed and who they review. You can manually add as many participants as you wish to any of the two tasks or delete them with the 'trash' icon.

Every time we choose a user from the drop-down menu the screen is updated. The indication *The submission has been successfully allocated* appears and a new name is added to the last place in the list. A last action is not necessary by means of the *Save* button, which is absent from this screen, and if we want to delete a participant all we have to do is click on the 'trash' icon that accompanies each one and confirm.

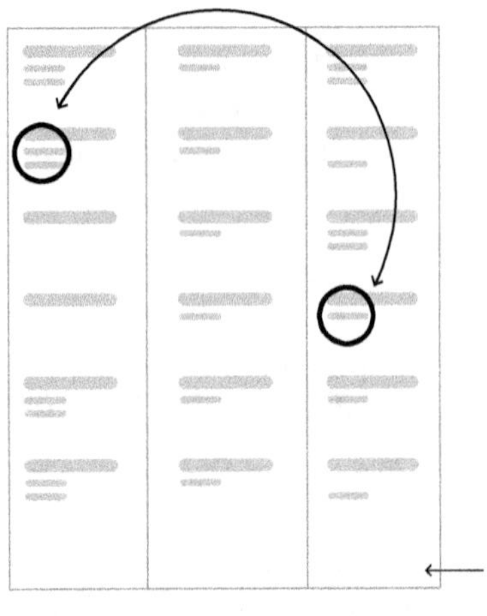

Each revision we add or delete **on either side is automatically reflected on the other one**, since assigning an evaluator to a submission (right column) always means –*viceversa*– assigning an evaluator to a submission (left column).

No 'Save' button, since updates are automatic

The *Manual allocation* allows us to generate allocations **even skipping the impositions of the group mode that we could have configured**. Thus, in a workshop with *Separate groups* mode we can only link participants from different groups by this method. Neither the random nor the scheduled one would allow it.

It is also particularly useful in cases where we know the participants personally and want to pair or group them by interest / language level / time slot, etc. However, before embarking on this laborious and time consuming work remember that there is already the utility of the 'groups'. For very small or manageable classes it can be interesting, but usually its only usefulness is to make adjustments or refine the other two systems.

Finally, let's remember that these allocation methods **can be used together by overlapping successively**. For example, we might want to first manually assign those four or five students or special cases that interest us and then fill in the rest of the allocations using the *Random* system and finally go back to manual and make the final retouches.

We are now ready to move on to the next phase, *Assessment*, where we give back to the students the leading role in this activity.

Assessment

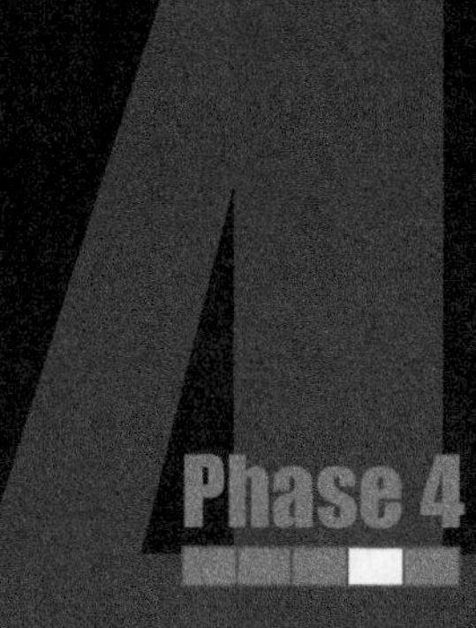

Teachers:
The protagonists here are, again, the students. As teachers, however, it is important to observe **how the rubric starts to behave**

Students:
They finally review their colleagues' exercises. While the phase is open they can also **enter again** to rectify those evaluations

4. Assessment phase

Students will finally be able to start assessing each other by applying the rubric or criteria we configured, as long as these three conditions are met together:

1. That we have **advanced the workshop** to this phase, *Assessment*, either manually by clicking on it or because we scheduled it in *Settings* (with that helpful button: «*Switch to the next phase after the submissions deadline*»)
2. That **there is no date/time deadlines enabled** in *Settings* for the start and/or end of such evaluations or, in case there is, that we are within it.
3. That we have **allocated them some tasks to evaluate**, of course, as we have just seen in the previous section, *Allocation*.

We are therefore aware of the chain of circumstances that must be in place for our students to be able to really begin their second half of the work. Although it may seem to us that we have fulfilled the three conditions, it never hurts to corroborate that this is really happening. If all goes well, they will see something like this:

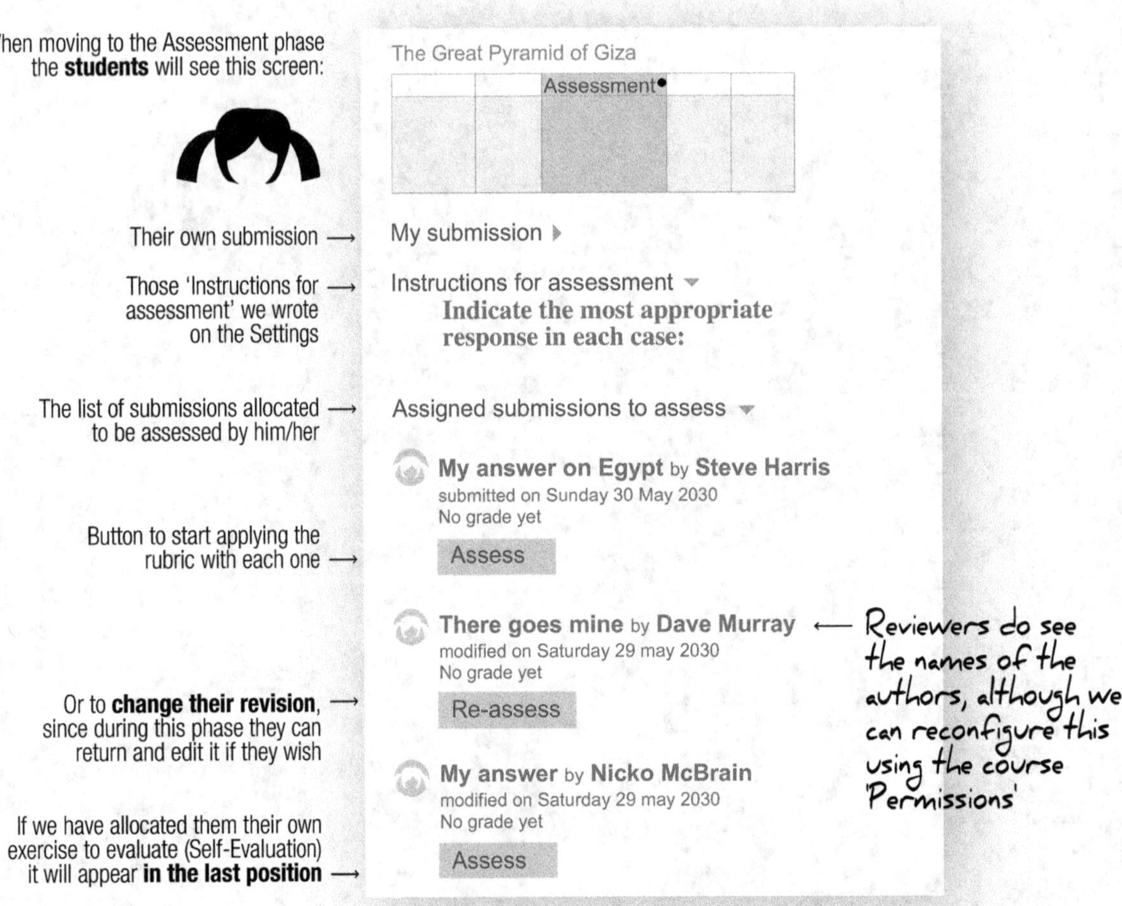

When moving to the Assessment phase the **students** will see this screen:

Their own submission →

Those 'Instructions for assessment' we wrote on the Settings →

The list of submissions allocated to be assessed by him/her →

Button to start applying the rubric with each one →

Or to **change their revision**, since during this phase they can return and edit it if they wish →

If we have allocated them their own exercise to evaluate (Self-Evaluation) it will appear **in the last position** →

← Reviewers do see the names of the authors, although we can reconfigure this using the course 'Permissions'

Teachers, on the other hand, see a very different screen below the control panel. It will now **show us in red** those allocations. They will **change to black** as students start filling them out.

The Great Pyramid of Giza

Sorting criteria (ascending / descending)

Direct access to each submission

Direct access to each review in detail

In black, those already completed

Name/Surname ▲▼	Submission/Last Modified ▲▼	Grades received	Grades given
ANA ALONSO	**There goes mine!!** modified on 30/05/2030...	⑦ < BELEN BOVEDA 6 < EVA EGUREN 7 < RUBEN RAMOS SAUL SEIJAS	EVA EGUREN 7 > SAUL SEIJAS 3 > BELEN BOVEDA
EVA EGUREN	**My response to this task** modified on 30/05/2030...	RUBEN RAMOS ANA ALONSO 6 < SAUL SEIJAS 5 < BELEN BOVEDA	6 > ANA ALONSO 6 > SAUL SEIJAS BELEN BOVEDA
BELEN BOVEDA	**I hope you enjoy mine** modified on 30/05/2030...	3 < ANA ALONSO EVA EGUREN SAUL SEIJAS 3 < RUBEN RAMOS	7 > ANA ALONSO 5 > EVA EGUREN 7 > SAUL SEIJAS
RUBEN RAMOS	No submission found for this user		7 > SAUL SEIJAS 7 > ANA ALONSO EVA EGUREN 3 > BELEN BOVEDA
SAUL SEIJAS	**Attached is my response** modified on 30/05/2030...	EVA EGUREN 7 < RUBEN RAMOS 7 < ANA ALONSO 7 < BELEN BOVEDA	ANA ALONSO EVA EGUREN BELEN BOVEDA

Saul hasn't started reviewing the others yet, while the rest have. In fact, Belen has already finished

Again, during this phase it is very important that we **sift through those first reviews as they come in** because we will discover, to our horror, that they are not applying our rubric as we had hoped. And, if we regret how we drafted it, it would still be possible to stop the process, fix the rubric and inform those first participants of any changes so they can re-start.

If this is the first time you put an assessment rubric in the hands of your students, **you may despair**. Even if we believe that its terms can no longer be clearer, the boundaries between categories cannot be better delineated and the margin for error can no longer be reduced... they will show you that yes, that, oh surprise, even the most objective – or objectifiable – aspects of the assessment can have different perspectives.

In fact, we may be in time to warn them and have them come in again to re-evaluate. First we saw that during the whole submission phase the students could re-enter and edit their answer or even delete it, in this case, during the assessment phase, they can also change their mind and re-enter to re-edit those votes as many times as they want —with that ***Re-assess button***– but **not to remove their participation** if they already saved it the first time.

Do students know who they are evaluating? (and *viceversa*)

By default Moodle is usually set up so that reviewers **do know who they are reviewing** but not the other way around, i.e. as evaluated they are not shown the name of the reviewers. The illustrations in this book are based on that standard. You can check your own workshop's settings by unfolding the cogwheel and clicking on the information section ***Check permissions***.

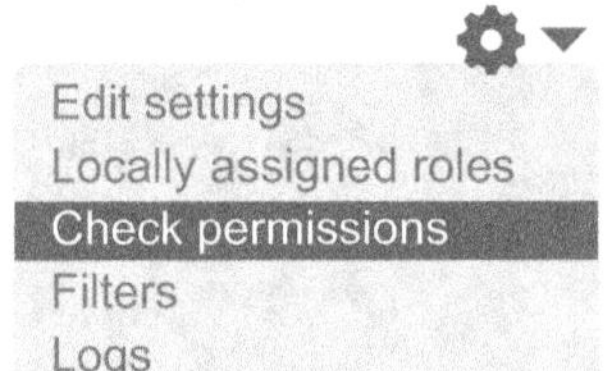

If you want to modify them, you will have to configure them at course level, if you have access to the ***Course Settings***, ***Participants*** section, ***Permissions*** section. There you will find all the available activities, including the Workshop, and you will be able to extend these privileges [**+** button] or restrict them [*Trash* button].

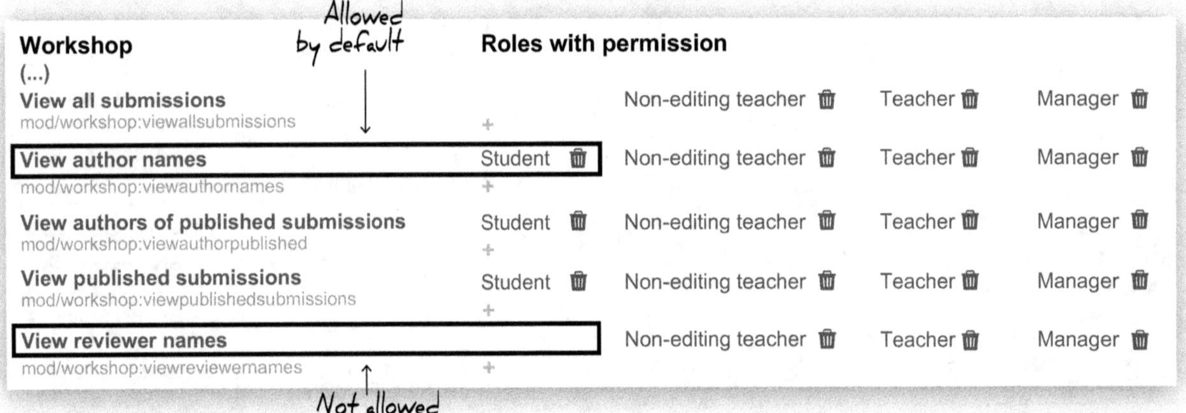

Workshop (...)	Allowed by default	Roles with permission		
View all submissions mod/workshop:viewallsubmissions	+	Non-editing teacher 🗑	Teacher 🗑	Manager 🗑
View author names mod/workshop:viewauthornames	Student 🗑 +	Non-editing teacher 🗑	Teacher 🗑	Manager 🗑
View authors of published submissions mod/workshop:viewauthorpublished	Student 🗑 +	Non-editing teacher 🗑	Teacher 🗑	Manager 🗑
View published submissions mod/workshop:viewpublishedsubmissions	Student 🗑 +	Non-editing teacher 🗑	Teacher 🗑	Manager 🗑
View reviewer names mod/workshop:viewreviewernames	+	Non-editing teacher 🗑	Teacher 🗑	Manager 🗑

My preference is to **keep the identities visible in both cases**. As the Spanish proverb says, «*the countryside cannot be closed off behind doors*». They all know each other —and even recognize their exercises, if not even by signing them by mistake–. Showing total transparency is a way to legitimize the process. The opposite strategy only serves to insinuate that they might cheat. While in this other way you turn that great enemy into your ally and, in fact, I encourage them to contact the authors and clear up any doubts. In the end, that feedback is often **precisely what we used to miss so much in the teaching and learning process**.

Not much more to do on our part during this phase. They are the protagonists here. We teachers are left to sit and observe with enormous intellectual vertigo how the process develops and how this kind of machine for producing knowledge that we have programmed works.

Grading

Teachers:
Finally we can check the detailed results, calculate and recalculate the scores by testing with different levels of exigency and monitor deviations

Students:
This phase in which we 'cook' the results is totally opaque to them. They will not have access to their grades until we 'close' the workshop

5. Grading phase

We finally reached the core problem of it all: how on earth all those peer-reviews that our students have carried out are converted into numbers. Because, with the exception of that workshop of the *Comments* type —which we saw that it ignores the numbers and serves as a mere dynamization of informal feedback between them— the usual thing will be this final output: those two numerical grades for each participant.

In this tricky section of the book it will be essential to follow this sequence:

1. We will learn to decode at a glance the abundant visual **information** shown on the screen. We will discover how what at first sight would seem an overwhelming amount of data is actually a road map as manageable as essential, and we will decipher the code it uses.

2. We will understand what **internal calculations** the platform is doing to award grades. We must know how does the machine operate, since we are delegating on it one of our essential tasks as teachers. If we dare with some basic statistics and we are not afraid of numbers we will feel much more confident when we rely on this system to accept their final grades or to proceed to modify them.

3. We will discover how we can control, modify, balance or **readjust these results manually**. One of the pillars of the workshop's legitimacy is the teacher's ability to supervise and redirect the process at all times and where this tutorial task will shine most brightly is in the final control of the grades.

The following disclaimer is addressed to Moodle: these peer-evaluation workshops are **not so much based on seeking total accuracy or absolute fairness** in each and every revision, but rather on aiming for a statistically acceptable result by increasing the sample size. That is, admitting that any grade —taken individually— will always be a more or less unpredictable mixture of justice and injustice, knowledge and ignorance, arbitrariness, good and bad faith, virtues and defects of each and every one of the participants. Admitting that we are decentralizing the very subjective task of assessing, our hope for obtaining the most adequate results possible is based on the accumulation of information and the perspective of the whole, rather than paying attention to concrete detail or trying to solve the whole case. That is why the tools we are going to describe below are designed so that the teacher can have **a global vision** of the whole activity that will allow him/her to later select **where to invest his/her time efficiently to correct locally the most serious or striking possible deviations**. Since it would be practically impossible to completely review all the information generated by the participants in those hundreds of allocations and thousands of calculations that have been needed.

1. Understanding the results grid:

Once the peer-assessments have been completed and we move on to this *Grading* phase, under the control panel we will be shown a very long list of results in six columns along a single page.

Make sure that your monitor offers enough horizontal space to display all six, otherwise the last ones on the right may be left out, especially in older versions of Moodle.

If stretching your browser window to the maximum is not possible either, a last trick is to reduce its display size (Keyboard shortcut 'Control +' to zoom in and 'Control -' to zoom out. Or 'Command' in the case of Apple keyboards)

< Ana receives from others   > Ana gives to others

Name / Surname	Submission / Last Modified	Grades **received**	Grade for submission (of 10)	Grades **given**	Grade for assessment (of 10)
ANA ALONSO	There goes mine!! modified on 30/05/2030...	9 (-)< BELEN BOVEDA 7 (-)< EVA EGUREN 7 (-)< SAUL SEIJAS 7 (-)< RUBEN RAMOS	-	5 (-)> EVA EGUREN 7 (-)> SAUL SEIJAS 3 (-)> BELEN BOVEDA	-
EVA EGUREN	My response to this modified on 30/05/2030...	9 (-)< RUBEN RAMOS 5 (-)< ANA ALONSO 6 (-)< SAUL SEIJAS 5 (-)< BELEN BOVEDA	-	7 (-)> ANA ALONSO 6 (-)> SAUL SEIJAS 3 (-)> BELEN BOVEDA	-
RUBEN RAMOS	*No submission found for this user*	-	-	7 (-)> SAUL SEIJAS 7 (-)> ANA ALONSO 9 (-)> EVA EGUREN 3 (-)> BELEN BOVEDA	-
BELEN BOVEDA	I hope you enjoy mine modified on 30/05/2030...	3 (-)< ANA ALONSO 3 (-)< EVA EGUREN SAUL SEIJAS 3 (-)< RUBEN RAMOS	-	9 (-)> ANA ALONSO 5 (-)> EVA EGUREN 7 (-)> SAUL SEIJAS	-
SAUL SEIJAS	Attached, my response modified on 30/05/2030...	6 (-)< EVA EGUREN 7 (-)< RUBEN RAMOS 7 (-)< ANA ALONSO 7 (-)< BELEN BÓVEDA	-	7 (-)> ANA ALONSO 6 (-)> EVA EGUREN BELEN BOVEDA	-

Showing 20 items per page   **Change... ◆**   300   400   500   ✓1,000

At the bottom we can change the number of lines we want to appear per page (called *items*) up to a maximum of 1,000.

Let's say your class is made up of fifty students and each one has to assess seven others. In that case, the results string will measure a whopping 350 lines of text, which you can scroll vertically in blocks of seven. In black the completed pair-evaluations and in red those others that, although assigned, have not been carried out.

If this is the first time you enter this phase, the grades will still be blank, uncalculated, so that's the first thing we'll do. By clicking on ***Recalculate grades*** the program will get a provisional grade for each student: one for his/her submission and the other for his/her assessments.

> Although the first drop-down menu on this page seems to offer different 'Rating Assessment Methods' to choose from, the only default option at present is '**Comparison with the best assessment**' –We will explain what this is later on–. Moodle seems to be planning to either extend the options in the future or allow developers to implement other methods, such as the *Most Weighted Grade Comparison* currently offered via www.moodle.org by Albert Gasset and David Pinyol Gras for Moodle versions 3.1 to 3.4.

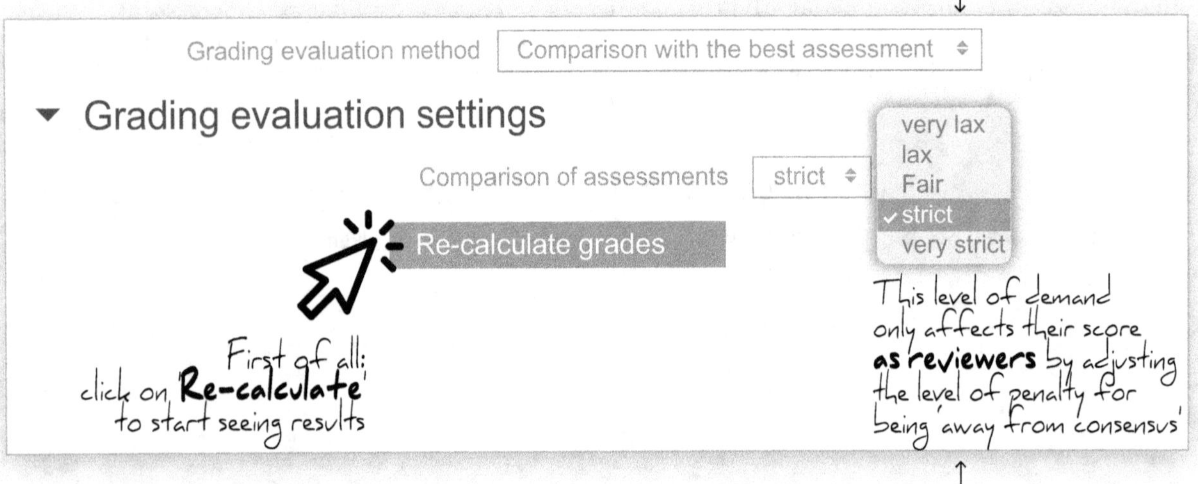

The second drop-down menu allows us to choose five levels of demand in the calculation of that mark for the evaluators, from *Very strict* to *Very lax* and the intermediate ones: *Strict*, *Fair* and *Lax*.

Choose any one of the five –for example, Very Lax– and click on *Recalculate grades*. Then, if you choose another one (*Very strict*) and recalculate again you will see that the **only changes will be in the right-hand area of the screen**, *Grade for assessment*, as this only affects the second of the two grades (the reviewer's grade). You can continue to try *Fair*, *Lax* and *Strict* to see what grades they get in that last column.

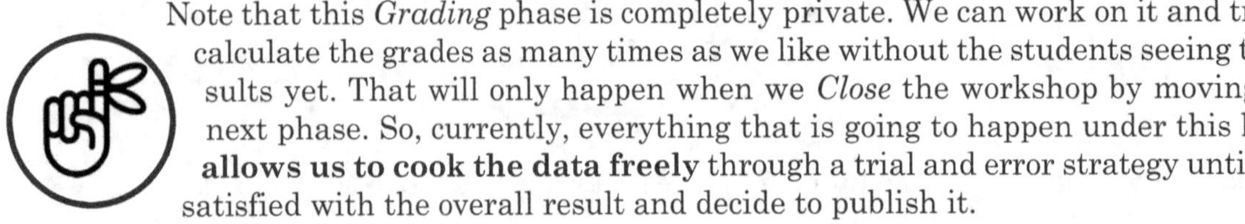

Note that this *Grading* phase is completely private. We can work on it and try to recalculate the grades as many times as we like without the students seeing their results yet. That will only happen when we *Close* the workshop by moving to the next phase. So, currently, everything that is going to happen under this heading **allows us to cook the data freely** through a trial and error strategy until we are satisfied with the overall result and decide to publish it.

After comparing the results of the five, stick with the one that you feel is most balanced at the moment or that best reflects the range of grades you would award.

The first column tells us the leading participant in each data set. For example, Ana Alonso in first place. The second column indicates whether that person has submitted an exercise or not and the date of the last modification. We can **directly access each submission** by clicking on its title. In the third one the difficulties begin. The title *Grades received*, indicates one by one –**in bold**– the grades given by each of her classmates. These figures are accompanied by another, in brackets, which refers to **the grade that this other colleague has received** for having reviewed in this way. The first one will therefore move in a certain range (for example, from zero to ten, as we set in the *Settings*) and the second one in the range we set for the Assessment (in the example of the image, from 0 to 10 as well).

In the next column –*Grade for submission*– and at a larger size, the first total grade, which is simply the **average of those received, which appeared in bold**. The amount of decimal places will be the one we indicated in the workshop *Settings*. We could still change it if we go back there.

The next column of data –*Grades given*– indicates one by one the grades that this particular student has given to the exercises of her classmates and next to each one, in parentheses, **the one that Anna takes** in each case. That is why **the one in bold is the second one**, because it is the one referred to this student, Ana, and whose total will crystallize in the following and last one: *Grade for assessment*, the total grade that our protagonist takes as an evaluator and that is again the arithmetic average of all her participations in those other panels. We will see below where these numbers come from.

Name / Surname	Submission / Last Modified	Grades received	Grade for submission (of 10)	Grades given	Grade for assessment (of 10)
ANA ALONSO	There goes mine!! modified on 30/05/2030...	9 (8,5)< BELEN BOVEDA 7 (5,8)< RUBEN RAMOS 7 (10)< EVA EGUREN 7 (9,1)< SAUL SEIJAS	**7,5** simple mean	5 (7,6)> EVA EGUREN 7 (8,2)> SAUL SEIJAS 3 (6,4)> BELEN BOVEDA	**7,4** simple mean
EVA EGUREN	My response to this modified on 30/05/2030...	9 (2,3)< RUBEN RAMOS 5 (7,6)< ANA ALONSO 6 (7,5)< SAUL SEIJAS 5 (3,1)< BELEN BOVEDA	6,3	7 (10)> ANA ALONSO 6 (10)> SAUL SEIJAS 3 (10)> BELEN BOVEDA	10,0
RUBEN RAMOS	*No submission found for this user*	-	-	7 (9,4)> SAUL SEIJAS 7 (5,8)> ANA ALONSO 9 (2,3)> EVA EGUREN 3 (7,7)> BELEN BOVEDA	6,3
BELEN BOVEDA	I hope you enjoy mine modified on 30/05/2030...	3 (6,4)< ANA ALONSO 3 (10)< EVA EGUREN SAUL SEIJAS 3 (7,7)< RUBEN RAMOS	3,0	9 (8,5)> ANA ALONSO 5 (3,1)> EVA EGUREN 7 (2,7)> SAUL SEIJAS	4,7
SAUL SEIJAS	Attached, my response modified on 30/05/2030...	6 (10)< EVA EGUREN 7 (9,4)< RUBEN RAMOS 7 (8,2)< ANA ALONSO 7 (2,7)< BELEN BOVEDA	6,8	7 (9,1)> ANA ALONSO 6 (7,5)> EVA EGUREN BELEN BOVEDA	8,3

In addition, each pair of numbers appears in a pro-
minent color as they work as a clickable link that
would allow us to access that particular evaluation
and see how each one has assessed or been assessed
in each section of the rubric.

In the Workshop module we do not have a button to conveniently download **all the submissions** as we are used to seeing in the 'Task' module of Moodle.

Belen is the only one who gave Anna a 'nine'. I'm curious about how she applied the rubric, I can check it by clicking on that specific evaluation made by Belen

Name / Surname	Submission / Last Modified	Grades received	Grade for sub-mission (of 10)	Grades given	Grade for asses-ment (of 10)
ANA ALONSO	There goes mine!! modified on 30/05/2030...	9 (8,5)< BELEN BOVEDA 7 (5,8)< RUBEN RAMOS 7 (10)< EVA EGUREN 7 (9,1)< SAUL SEIJAS	7,5	5 (7,6)> EVA EGUREN 7 (8,2)> SAUL SEIJAS 3 (6,4)> BELEN BOVEDA	7,4

Note how it is also possible to sort all this information vertically —**using these little grey trian-gles**— according to the column that interests us the most (*First name, Last name, Date Sent, Date Last Modified, Grade for submission or Grade for assessment*). Both up and down. Thus, we may prefer to start by analyzing them alphabetically, but we might be more interested in star-ting from 'best work submitted' (or worst), or from 'best student assessing' (or worst), etc.

For this case (choosing that level of demand in the task of evaluating) it is very interesting to order the columns according to the *Grade for assessment*, to see which students get the best grade as reviewers and how many there are in that area, and
viceversa: which students get the worst grade and how many of them fall into that poor
area of this ranking. In this way, we can also observe the results of the different levels
of demand (*Lax... Fair*, etc.).

Other symbols on the grid

The results grid can also show ats [@], studs [✗] and different colors in the grades.
These are explained at the end of this chapter. First we need to look more closely at how
these grades are calculated and how we can change them.

2. How those two grades are calculated:

Grade for submission

The first one should be familiar to us, since we have been building it manually when designing that evaluation format or rubric.

Starting with the maximum score that we left assigned in the *Settings* (for example, twenty points), then throughout the rubric we established the relative weighting of each criterion –and within each of these, that of each level–. We didn't even have to worry about these sections adding up to twenty points as well. Moodle already adjusted them proportionally as we introduced new ones or removed others.

Then each student has been assessed by applying that same rubric, which is a tool to facilitate the translation of others' opinions into numerical values without having to worry about deciding on grades.

And since finally the total grade for the submission is, again, a simple arithmetic mean of all those aggregates, it could be said that the only thing Moodle is doing here is saving us the hassle of adding up all the grades in each subsection, weighting them correctly and, one by one, calculating the averages. Nothing new, then.

With the only exception we saw for the *Number of errors* grading strategy, which allowed us to build a custom *Grade mapping table* that modified the results curve as we saw fit, in most cases this Grade by Submission is the same procedure of any teacher who **passes on his students' grades on a piece of paper or an Excel sheet**.

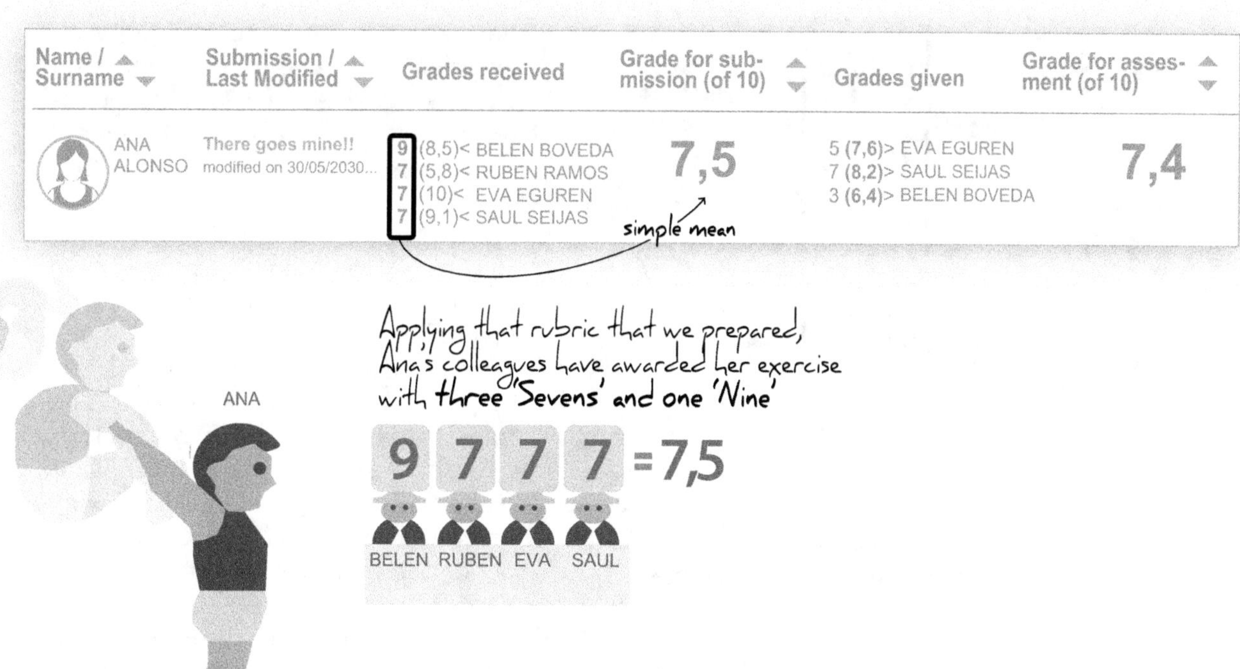

Name / Surname	Submission / Last Modified	Grades received	Grade for submission (of 10)	Grades given	Grade for assessment (of 10)
ANA ALONSO	There goes mine!! modified on 30/05/2030...	9 (8,5)< BELEN BOVEDA 7 (5,8)< RUBEN RAMOS 7 (10)< EVA EGUREN 7 (9,1)< SAUL SEIJAS	7,5	5 (7,6)> EVA EGUREN 7 (8,2)> SAUL SEIJAS 3 (6,4)> BELEN BOVEDA	7,4

Grade for assessment

This one is a bit more laborious. How does Moodle '*judge the judge*'? Let's see how those other ratings, which **are in parentheses**, are calculated.

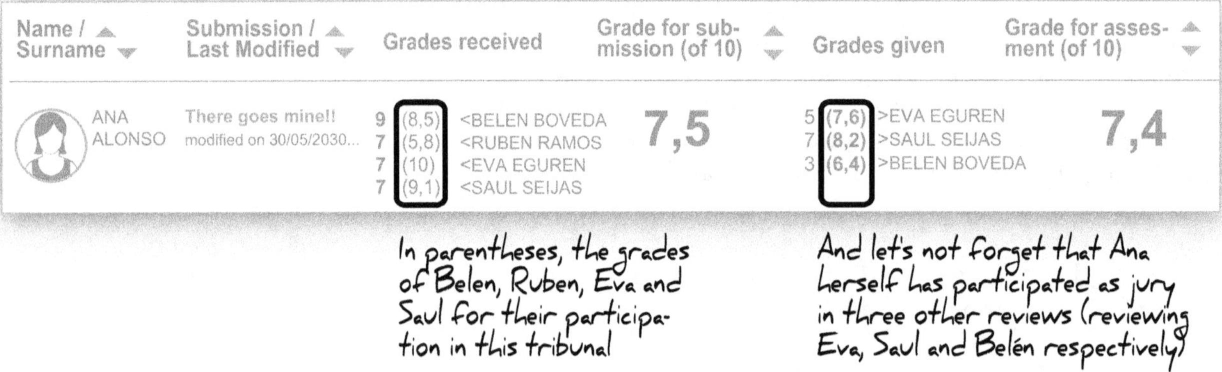

In parentheses, the grades of Belen, Ruben, Eva and Saul for their participation in this tribunal

And let's not forget that Ana herself has participated as jury in three other reviews (reviewing Eva, Saul and Belén respectively)

Short answer: To rate the evaluation work of each judge we have to imagine him or her as part of a court. First Moodle calculates mathematically what the 'consensus' rating of those judges is, and then it will penalize each juror **as they move away from that consensus more or less**. Regardless of whether he or she is awarding a grade above or below that, it is the difference that is penalized.

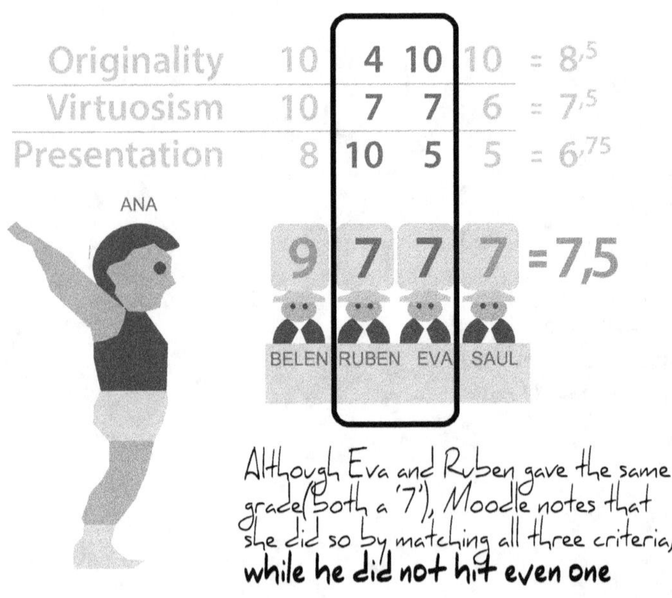

Although Eva and Ruben gave the same grade (both a '7'), Moodle notes that she did so by matching all three criteria, **while he did not hit even one**

But then, why do two students who have awarded the same grade for an exercise –for example, Ruben and Eva, who gave Anna a 7– then get different grades for that assessment? –Ruben gets a 5.8 while Eva gets a 10–.

Because Moodle doesn't make these calculations on that overall grade given, but by taking into account one by one each criterion in which we know the rubric is broken down. The important thing is not, therefore, that hypothetical 'seven' (global) that Ruben and Eva gave, but 'how' they arrived at that score. How they responded to each criterion.

Ana's exercise was very good in Originality and somewhat weaker in Presentation. Although all four juries awarded very similar overall scores, Moodle is very attentive to details, so it didn't go unnoticed that Ruben was being a very weak reviewer.

And likewise, let's remember the **weightings**, because in the final grade one criterion could weigh more than others, depending on the relative weight we established in each one, in which case it will also penalize proportionally more or less.

Suddenly we can notice that the number of mathematical calculations performed by Moodle is growing exponentially. For example, in **a classroom of 50 students** where each of them assesses seven other (that's 350 reviews) with a rubric consisting in four criteria, we should calculate 1,400 means and against each of them compare the seven participants –9,800 partial results– also taking into account 1,400 standard deviations and then distribute them again among the students (to the 50 evaluated, their averages and to the reviewers, the averages of their respective seven penalties). All this without considering the weighting of each section of the rubric. Conclusion: It would be impossible for us teachers to sit down and do **these 10,000 accounts** – much less repeat them five times to see if a *Lax, Strict,* or *Very Strict* strategy would be more appropriate for us...– if it was not for the support of computer-assisted methods such as this one.

When I hear comments such as «...*Oh, yes, peer-assessment... I already do that in my classes by passing them a questionnaire on paper so that they can check the exercises of the others...*» I better hold my tongue. A genuine co-evaluation that also aims to ensure that peers can reliably grade each other **can only take place using computer-assisted methods**. Any attempt to emulate it analogically is a laudable attempt to teach better, but it not only demands a greater organisational effort on the part of the teacher, but ends up giving him or her a greater qualifying role as –precisely– a hetero-controller over the process, since it will now require him or her to supervise both tasks, those of delivery on the one hand and those of review on the other. Which seems to be a big contradiction.

Let us continue to qualify our rating by the *Assessment*.

Although in this example we have for instance numerical grades –with our fictitious Eva giving a 10, a 7 and a 5 respectively to each of the three criteria–, remember that in practice she will almost never choose these numbers freely, but will simply click on the teacher's rubric, with its sections fixed and without knowing her score – for example *'Poor=0', 'Fair=3', 'Good=7'* and *'Excellent=10'*–. But if Moodle is going to penalise someone for their deviation from the 'consensus' and it turns out that this consensus between several raters (the average they give) will almost always end up being a value with decimals, somewhere between two options (let's say 6.75) then no reviewer really had the chance to select it and make the perfect assessment because their only alternatives were fixed to only those four: 0, 3, 7 and 10.

This is the time to start nuancing what until here had been the short answer, as the software goes even deeper:

Moodle starts from the mathematical calculation of the consensus (let's put that average of 6.75 in a certain criterion, such as 'Presentation') but then it makes the result more flexible by moving it to 'the answer closest to it', which it takes as ***Best assessment*** (in this case, Good '7' would be the closest). And that is the one to which it gives the full mark. So that is how the differences are actually calculated. Not compared to the 6.75 but to the '7'.

For example, let's continue with this example: the teacher sets a four-level scale [0, 3, 7 and 10] from '*Bad*' [zero points], '*Fair*' [three], '*Good*' [seven] and finally '*Excellent*' [ten]. If of the members of a fictitious jury –let's say seven students– four give a 'Good' and the other three an 'Excellent', the consensus grade, the average, would be somewhere between seven and ten, specifically 8.3 (for a total of 58 points divided among 7 jurors). In this case, slightly closer to seven ('Good') than to ten ('Very Good'), so that he considers that the *Best possible assessment* was 'Good'. Then, not the 8.3 of the average 'consensus', but the one closest to it among the four limited options that the reviewers had to choose from in the closed section. This is why Moodle gives these four users a full mark, because they evaluated as closely as they could from among the closed options offered to them. The software then compares the score given by the other three evaluators against this 'best possible' score to penalise them for the difference.

What scope of action does the reviewer have in awarding a grade?

Depending on the four type of workshop. All examples from 0 to 10

Accumulative grading	Comments	Number of errors	Rubric
?	**10**	**10** "Right"	**10** "Excellent"
In the 'Scale' type Aspects the reviewers choose which grade to give. Any integer, no decimals	The mere fact of reviewing awards the maximum grade	Only binary options. All or nothing	**7** "Good" The values of each level was previously fixed by the teacher **3** "Regular"
		0 "Wrong"	**0** "Bad"
10 alternatives (in this example)	No alternative	2 alternatives	4 alternatives (in this example)

It is therefore possible for them to get 'full' marks and, in fact, it is often more common than teachers would sometimes like.

Because, what happens if there is a tie or that consensus score is exactly in the middle, at the same distance, of two different options? If, for example, there are eight jurors equally distributed: two give a 'Bad', two a 'Fair', two a 'Good' and the last two an 'Excellent', the average would be exactly 5, equidistant from 'Fair' and 'Good', so Moodle considers —easy solution— that all of these four students in the intermediate zone have 'the best assessment'. It opts for what's best for students, which is **to consider both assessments as 'best' and awards them all with the highest mark**.

It is often the case that the consensus score (average) is right between two others. In this situation, Moodle considers both to be 'the best assessment'.

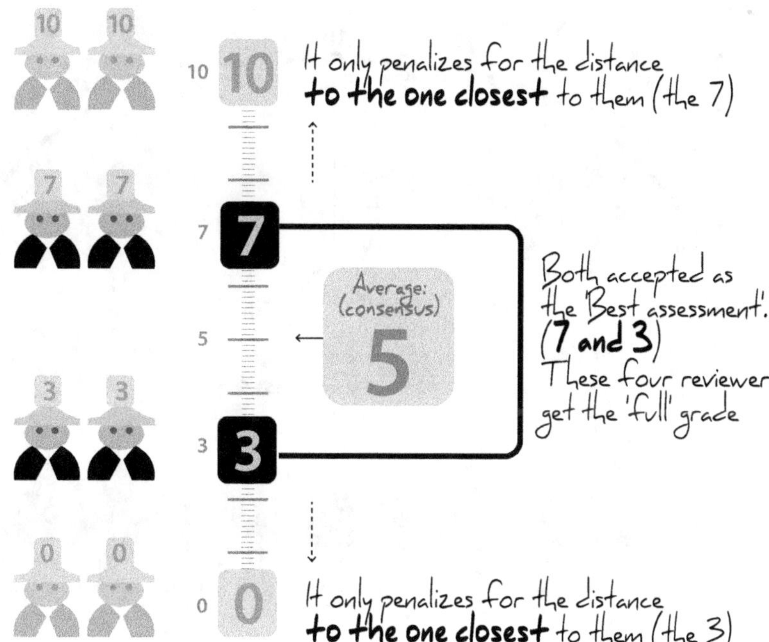

And in the same way, when calculating how far the other four assessors have moved away from each other, those at the extremes – that distance with the best possible assessment – he chooses to benefit them **by comparing it with the one closest to each other**. The two evaluators who gave an 'Excellent' [10] will only be penalized for moving slightly away from the 'Good' [7] because it is the 'Best evaluation' that is closest to them, and the same underneath for the other two evaluators, who gave a 'Bad' [0], will only be penalized for their distance from the 'Regular' [3], which is the one that is closest to them.

The same happens in case of ties. If for example two equidistant blocks are generated: let's say that half of the eight evaluators had chosen the same score and the other four had chosen another one —any of them—, automatically all of the participants, all eight, would have a 'full' as evaluators in that criterion for being at the same distance from the average.

This is how the demand curve works

When we choose one of these five levels, from *Very Lax* to *Very Strict*, we are grading the penalties **to the reviewers**. In this fictitious example eleven reviewers have given totally different grades to Ana —from zero to ten, all possibilities— so her average is a five. That '5' for Ana does not change, but let's see what happens to the one each of them receives for their evaluation:

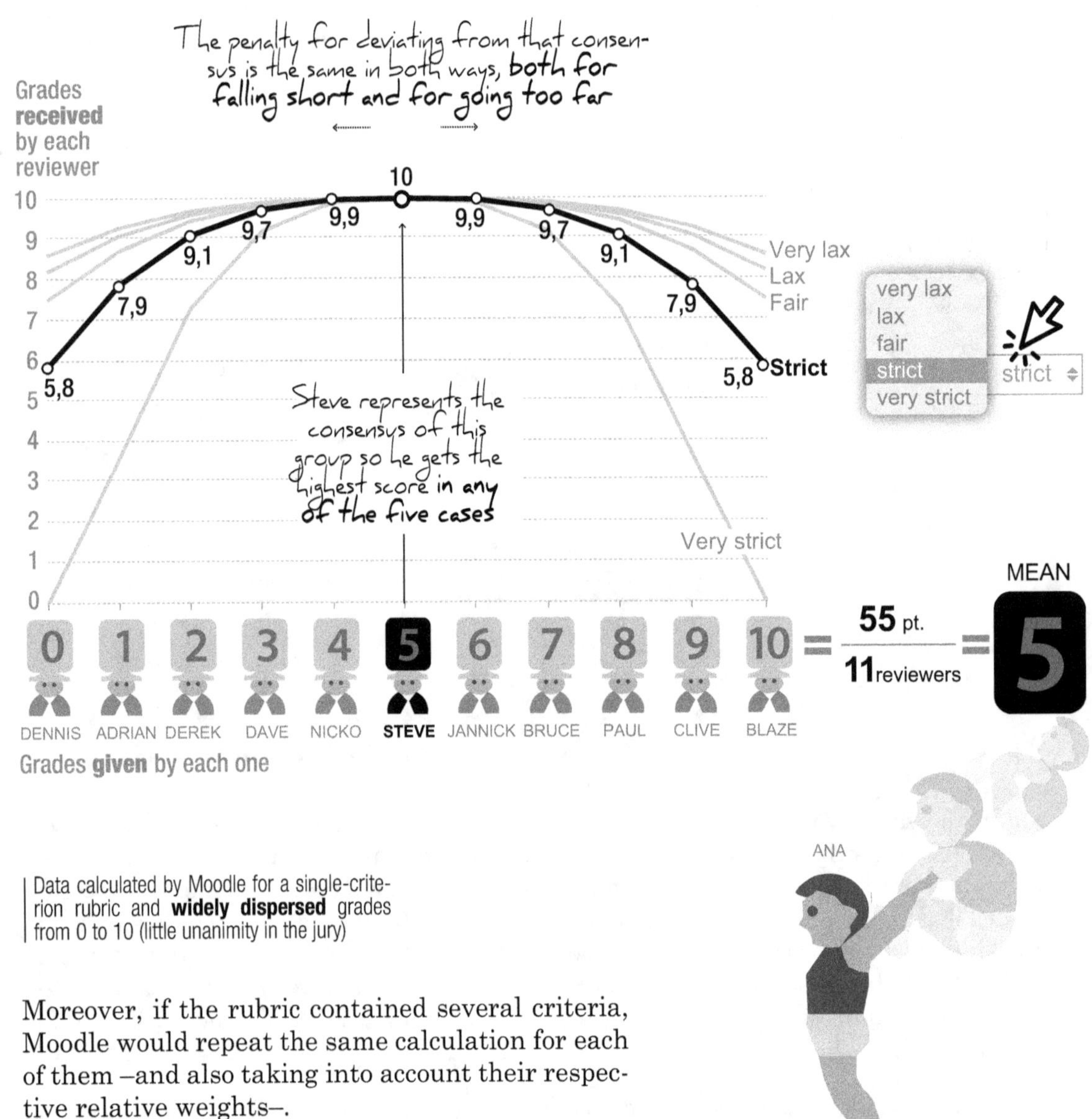

| Data calculated by Moodle for a single-criterion rubric and **widely dispersed** grades from 0 to 10 (little unanimity in the jury)

Moreover, if the rubric contained several criteria, Moodle would repeat the same calculation for each of them —and also taking into account their respective relative weights—.

On the other hand, each of these reviewers will have assessed many other colleagues in addition to Ana, so that their final assessment rating will be **the average of those obtained** in all these court appearances.

And this is how the unanimity of this consensus has influence

But Moodle doesn't just compare the rest against this 'best possible evaluation', it also takes into consideration **what this consensus looks like**, i.e. the dispersion of these values. When the standard deviation was high (as in the example above, where the eleven jurors gave disparate scores) it was less penalising to be far away. Let us now see how things change when there is greater unanimity among reviewers.

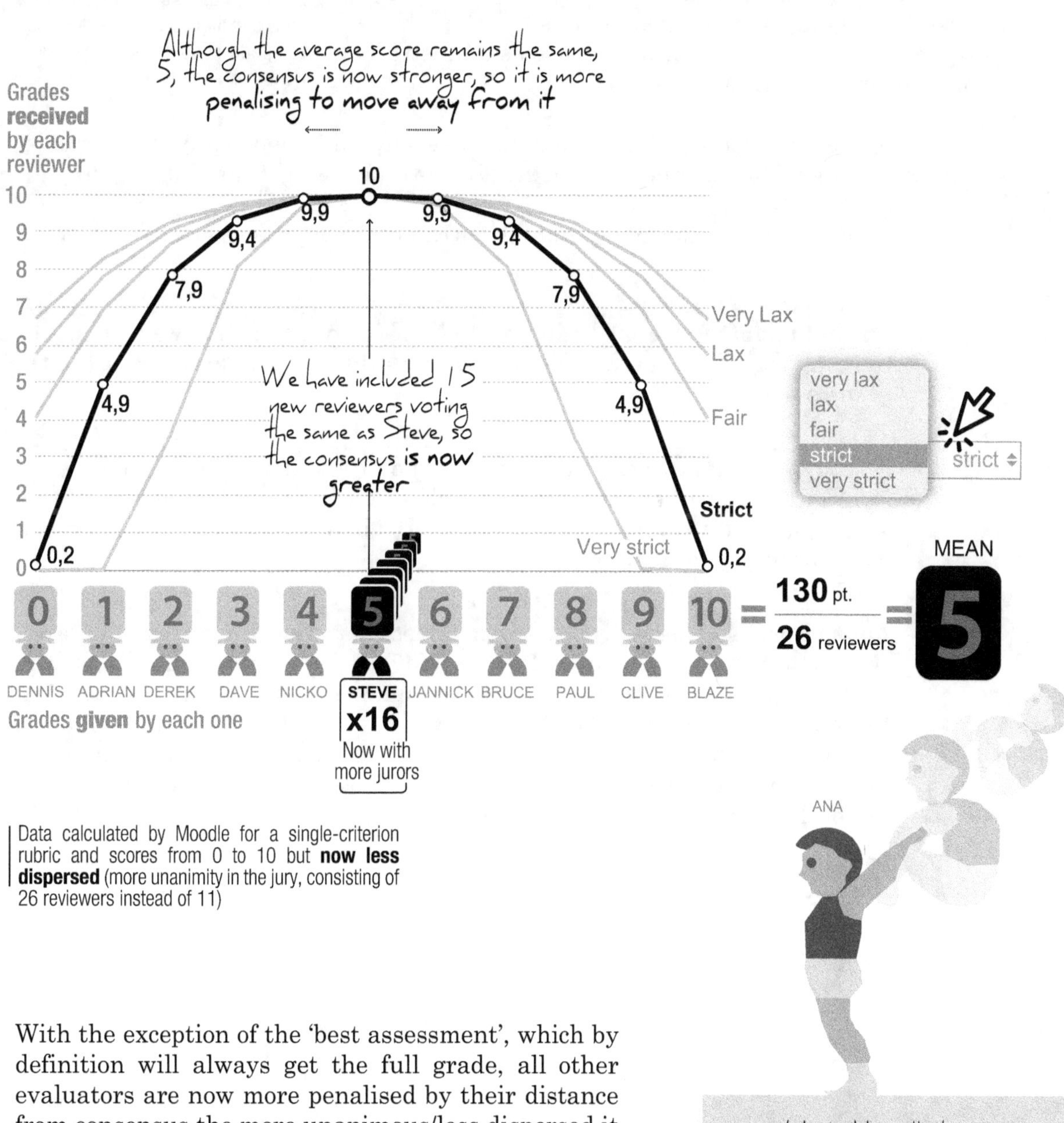

Data calculated by Moodle for a single-criterion rubric and scores from 0 to 10 but **now less dispersed** (more unanimity in the jury, consisting of 26 reviewers instead of 11)

With the exception of the 'best assessment', which by definition will always get the full grade, all other evaluators are now more penalised by their distance from consensus the more unanimous/less dispersed it is. The new 'Strict' curve on this page **would seem to be equivalent to the 'Very Strict' curve on the previous page**, for scattered values.

So there's little point in assigning only two evaluators per submission?

That's right. In fact, from a grading point of view, **there is none**. By definition, if there are only two evaluations and we do the arithmetic average between them, they will always be the same distance —mathematically— from that average. So they will always get that 'full mark'. It loses any discriminatory effectiveness. It will only serve, of course, to score the other student's submission, but it has no use as an instrument to evaluate the assessors.

So, if you decide to allocate only two evaluators per submission, then **any rating you give for this effort will be a 'highest mark' for all participants**. Being aware of this, you may decide that you should indicate 'zero points' for this work in the main settings and that 100% of each student's grade should come exclusively from their submission.

Note that even if you assign three evaluators to each submission, if any of them leaves this task incomplete that would be enough for the other two get the 100% again.

From the above, some **practical conclusions** can be drawn when setting up a workshop:

- The minimum number of evaluators valid if you are going to award points for the evaluation is **three**, but **the more you allocate, the more reliable the results** will be.

- Although we cannot avoid draws within the jury, it is possible to adopt small strategies to at least slightly reduce the chances of draws occurring —such as assigning an **odd number** of evaluators per submission (or an even number if you add the self-evaluation).

- Another one is to design rubrics with values that, when added together, avoid results that are multiples of each other. Why not choose **prime numbers** whenever possible? For example, if you were thinking of establishing four levels in this progressive sequence: 0/3/6/12, you could replace it with this other 0/3/7/13, which keeps some sections almost proportional to the previous ones but, as you can realise, makes it difficult to produce arithmetic averages equidistant to any two of the limits in their different combinations.

3. Monitoring and modifying grades:

This phase of supervision is the one that none of us would like to have to carry out. In fact, if it were the case that all your instructions for submission and your evaluation rubric had been clear and no misunderstandings had occurred and all participants were mature enough, and equable –with no personal interest in inflating their grade, or that of others, or in reducing it among themselves–, if all of these circumstances were present together, this phase of supervision would be superfluous. (Well, and even the teacher himself would almost be in excess as well). But let's be realistic, that hypothetical and idyllic harmony will never happen. In practice, **a little police work will always be sadly indispensable from here** on in.

The all-powerful teacher will have to come down from Heaven and intervene in various ways with his Divine Hand to redirect the possible injustices or deviations caused by the co-evaluation between peers.

Let us see how this is possible:

1. Breaking into courts where we believe that unfair assessments are taking place in order to **provide our own binding opinion**
2. Retouching **grades received by the reviewers** or even grading them directly manually
3. **Weighing** up the best evaluators –or eliminating the worst–
4. Removing problematic **submissions**

However, given that peer-evaluation using Moodle involves a large number of subjects and a series of multiple pairs and combinations, at this point the number of possible variables is so high that **it would be impossible to fully monitor** –even in minimal detail– **the entire process**.

For this reason, almost as important as knowing how to rectify and modify results or scores manually will be learning to detect first the most flagrant or general possible deviations. That is, optimizing our time dedicated to supervision –which is limited– by looking at the overall picture, focusing on the improvements we can make systematically or more globally, and leaving isolated cases for a second review.

In addition, if you are familiar with the Moodle **Gradebook** you know that it is also possible to manually rewrite any student's grade or exclude it from the total course count. Now, let's use that method **only as a last resort**, because although it would be very fast and convenient for us we would not be overriding the other side effects that that assessment may have had on other students' grades as well, so it is advisable to correct it first, at the source, at the beggining, rather than at the end.

We will have to give up covering as many cases as possible and sacrifice the details. That is why we are also going to explain these methods of monitoring from more general to more particular. In the same order in which they should be applied.

Red and black blocks:

With our first visual review we are going to mitigate possible injustices derived from this system of simple arithmetic averages. Remember that both the grade received for the exercise and the grade received for the evaluation are based on the average of others, even if it was only ONE.

Let's start with the **left zone: column of *Grades received***. It is very common to find assignments in both black (completed) and red (incomplete). This simply means that of the —let's say nine— jurors who should have evaluated the submission of a participant, one has failed. Here it is **not the fault of that student** that someone else did not do his or her duty. Let us simply be on the alert in case the repeated absence of jurors distorts the result. If the number of nine reviewers is reduced to five, we could still be satisfied, but if it falls even lower —3?— we may have to consider breaking as substitute evaluators both to readjust the qualification that this task deserves and also —of course— to balance the evaluators' own qualification. We will soon see how.

We know that if the number of evaluators is reduced, the grade is quickly distorted. But, in addition, if a submission is evaluated **by only TWO people**, both would automatically receive 100% as evaluator, no matter how disparate or unfair their criteria were.

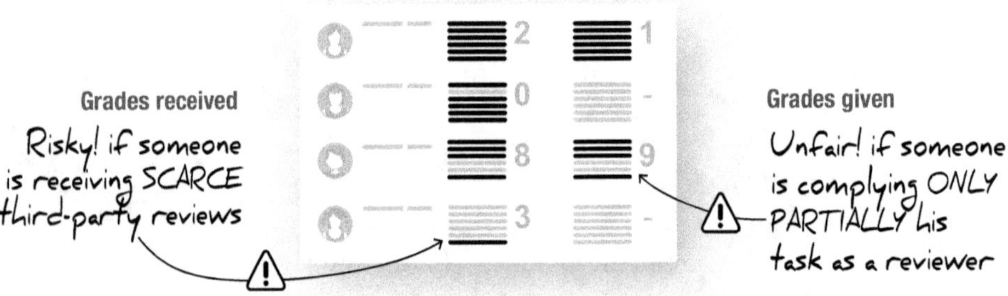

On the contrary, in the **right zone**, column of ***Grades given***. The usual thing should be that each student, one of two: **either has evaluated all** the submissions that were assigned to them —we see all their text rows in black, so his grade will be the average of those obtained as an evaluator— **or they have not reviewed any** —we see all them in red, in which case they get a zero in this part of the exercise—. But, what if someone has only partially completed their obligations and has not assessed all of them, or worse, has assessed only one? Well, let's remember that the system would go unnoticed, because it takes the simple average and if someone had evaluated only one, Moodle would take directly and without almost any effort that single grade obtained as an evaluator (perhaps a 100%?). And **in spite of having skipped the rest of their obligations**. Soon we will see how to modify their grade so that they get the one they really deserve.

On the right column it should be fulfilled that all the assignments appear **completed** (in black, those who have evaluated the others) **or incomplete** (in red, because they have not carried out this second part of the exercise at all)

A quick vertical review will help us to detect these anomalies. What we are looking for is that each block is uniformly made up of a single color: either black text because they are allocations that have been completed or red text (assignments that have not been evaluated, either because the participants were lazy, or because the deadline was closed before they finished, etc.) and they do not have a grade. But we will soon get our hands on the rest of the cases, with mixed colors.

Worst and best reviewers (and lazy ones):

The second step is to sort the right column, *Grade for assessment*, from lowest to highest –that is, from lowest to highest mark– and automatically highlight at the top of the ranking those reviewers who are evaluating their peers by moving further away from the consensus. This may be due to factors as diverse as lack of knowledge, bad intentions, lack of time, misinterpretation of instructions or even sometimes, on the contrary, an excess of knowledge –because they are students who have simply assessed 'differently' than their peers or at least moving away from the consensus, and perhaps rightly so–.

And in the lower zone, on the contrary, those other students who are evaluating their colleagues particularly well. It's probably just that. Here the casuistry boils down to, quite simply, **those who have done best**. At least my experience, having completed multiple workshops, **is that this result is by far the most reliable**.

Once we have located both groups at the extremes, we will soon see how quickly we can use that information to improve the overall result.

A separate case is that of those other students –maybe lazy ones?– who could have limited themselves to filling rubrics in a systematic and disrespectful way (all tens, all fives, all zeros...) and who could have gone unnoticed because they were scattered in any other area of this ranking. With a quick review of the awarded marks –**the figures outside the parenthesis**– we will look for these anomalous patterns that will give them away.

We will also see how to track other, more subtle, deviations, but first we will learn how to correct these, as the method will be similar later on for the rest of them.

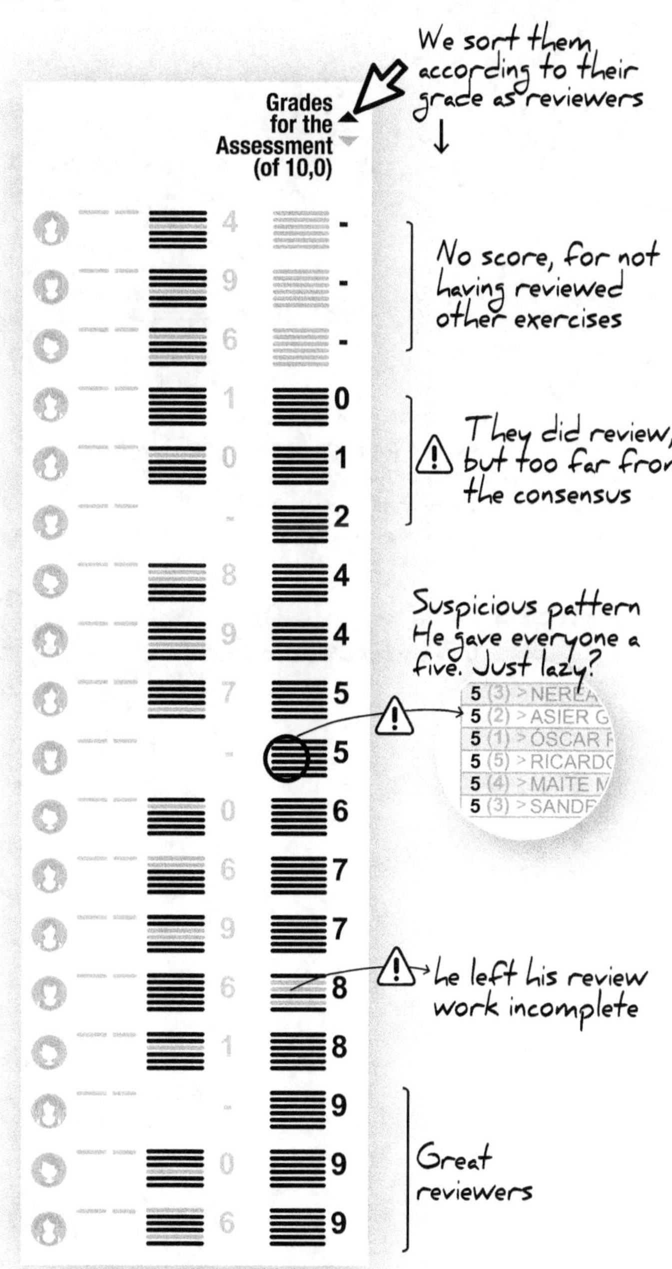

Modifying the grades:

I see that not only did Belen submit quite a poor exercise –awarded a 3– but now, worse still, I suspect that she also seems to have taken the evaluation of her peers to heart – mark: 2.1–. So I will look at what she has done with Saul's exercise in case it was not as correct as it should be. When you click on the grades –those numbers act as links– you get **a screen like the one below**.

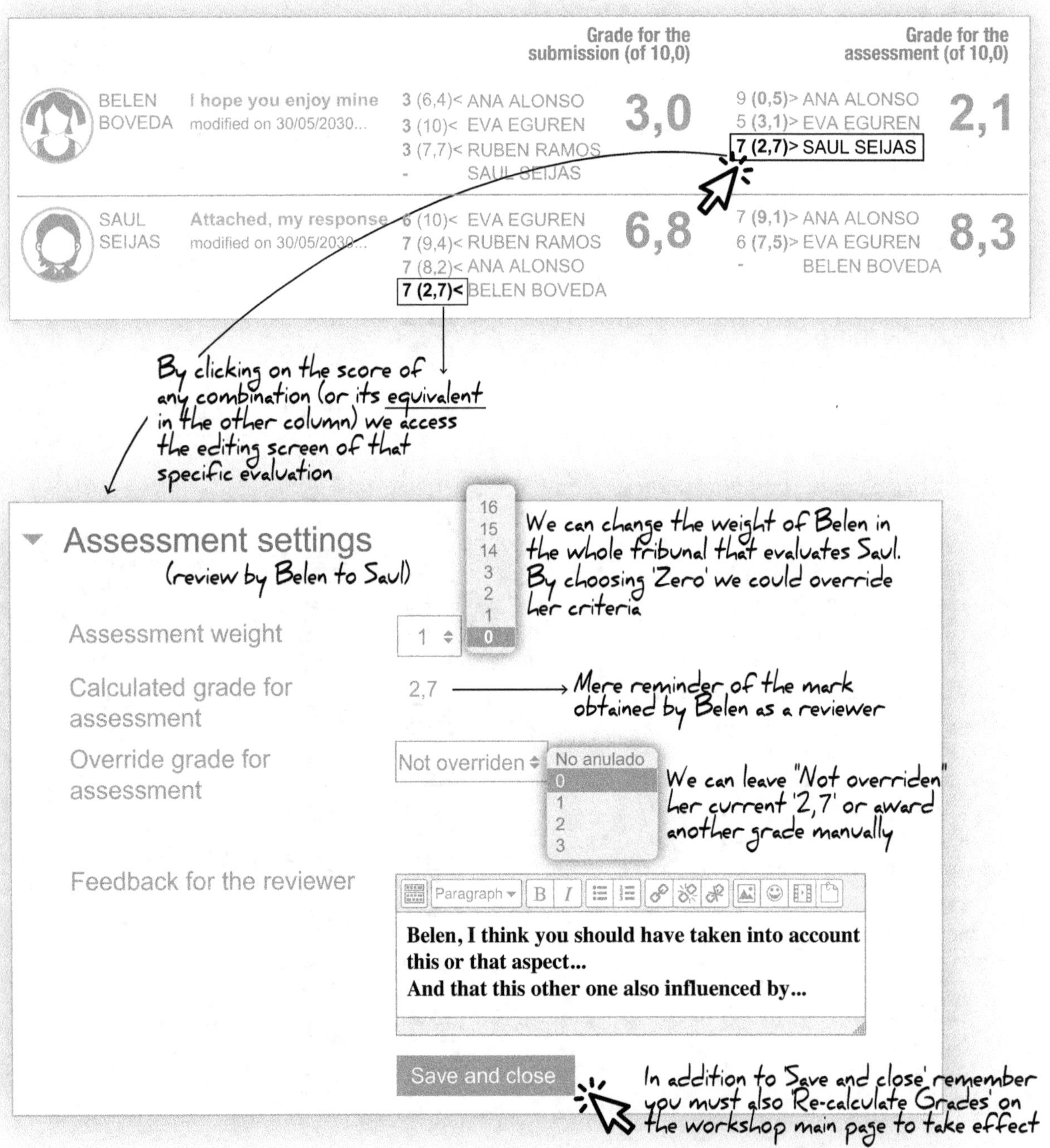

By clicking on the score of any combination (or its equivalent in the other column) we access the editing screen of that specific evaluation

We can change the weight of Belen in the whole tribunal that evaluates Saul. By choosing 'Zero' we could override her criteria

Mere reminder of the mark obtained by Belen as a reviewer

We can leave "Not overriden" her current '2,7' or award another grade manually

In addition to 'Save and close' remember you must also 'Re-calculate Grades' on the workshop main page to take effect

In it, and under the title *Assessed Submission* we see the exercise first –with that *Title* freely assigned by the author to his submission, author, date and time–. Secondly, the evaluation made by his colleague, and the name of the evaluator and total grade. The complete rubric, criterion by criterion, as it was filled in by the reviewer. And finally, under the heading **Assessment settings**, [Illustration above] our chance to get our hands on this mess with the following options:

Assessment weight: this refers to how much weight this particular jury should have in the panel. By default, 'one'. If, for example, there are seven people who have assessed this submission, in principle they all have the same weight in the final average mark awarded to the exercise (one seventh) but if we consider that this reviewer is not judging correctly and it would be fairer to disregard his assessment we can reduce his weighting to 'zero', so that now the final average mark of the exercise submitted by that other person will be calculated by counting only the other six.

And if, on the contrary, this assessment seems so correct to us that it should be the pattern for all the other jurors to follow, we can overweight it by double, triple, quadruple... (up to a maximum of x16, so that the new total average score would be computed as if there were 22 people evaluating –instead of those seven– since this jury would now weigh no more and no less than 16) and the other six as one each. Again, this decision would also alter the grade of the evaluated exercise.

Note: this weighting always refers to the **review as a whole**, (all the criteria of the rubric in question) so if we are going to raise the weighting of an evaluator we must be careful and be sure that all her decisions have indeed been the right ones and the rubric he filled in –in full– is perfect.

Calculated grade for assessment: In this section we are only informed of the grade this reviewer is receiving as an evaluator. Note that this number was calculated before we modified his or her 'weighting' in the previous section. If we had done so, it is possible that this grade would have changed under the new circumstances (especially if there were few evaluators in total for this submission and therefore their relative weight would have become much lower or higher) and therefore, if we are interested in knowing exactly the new grade we should refresh the result (*Save and Close* button), click on *Recalculate grades* and then enter again.

Override grade for assessment: Here we can choose between keeping this evaluator's original score as a juror (*Not overriden*) or manually awarding any other using the drop-down menu. Before manually changing her evaluation grade, remember that by simply removing her from the jury (weight: 'zero') we are slightly penalising her –reducing her *Grade for the Assessment*–

It only allows **integers, no decimals**. So if the evaluation was worth a maximum of, say, two points the options here would be just those three: '0, 1 and 2'.

as she moves further away from the new consensus. And *viceversa*, that if we are weighting it up we were also moving the consensus grade towards the opinion of this jury and therefore indirectly rewarding her. All this in this specific case (her revision to Saul). Let us remember that Belen has also participated in other tribunals (such as Eva's and Ana's) and her mark as an evaluator is the average of the three. Here we have arranged only one of them.

Having seen the options on that screen you can already deduce how it will serve us to correct these first anomalies that we have mentioned.

Adjusting the evaluation of the 'worst' reviewers:

Now that we know that we can change the weight –up or down– of the assessment that one student has given to any other's exercises, let's go back to that inverted ranking of evaluators to apply a series of quite intuitive adjustments.

Let's see: we have at the top those students who are the 'worst' evaluating. There will be blatant cases and others not so clear. For example, students with a very low grade evaluating and also corroborated by another grade also very poor in their exercise, or worse: they did not submit. If we add to this the fact that sometimes we know personally the trajectory of some of them, we can already **consider pruning directly all their assessments** for the good of their classmates, who would be receiving unfair grades.

Since Moodle is sometimes a bit slow to open and close windows and here we need to open seven at once to make only a small adjustment to each one, a very advisable trick is to press the '**Control**' (or 'Command' in Mac) key **at the same time as you click on each link**.

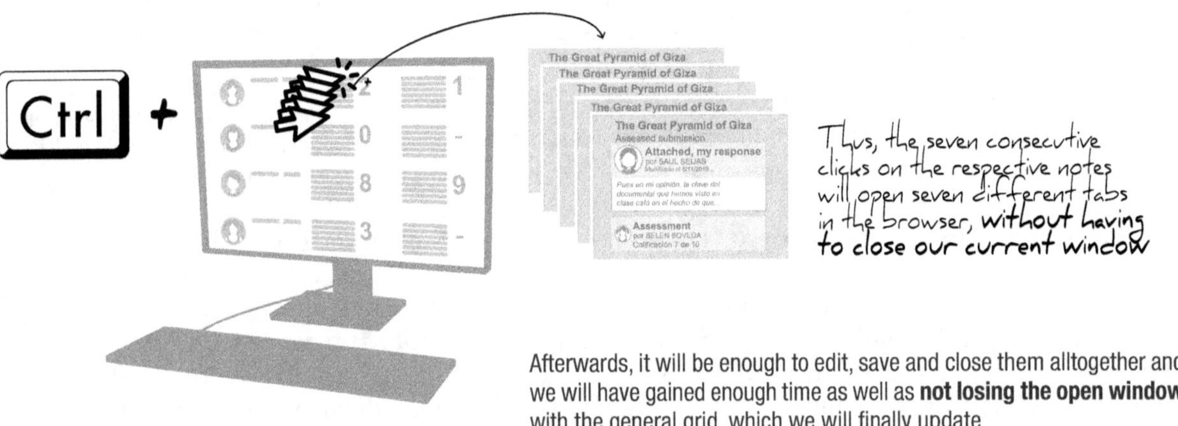

Thus, the seven consecutive clicks on the respective notes will open seven different tabs in the browser, without having to close our current window

Afterwards, it will be enough to edit, save and close them alltogether and we will have gained enough time as well as **not losing the open window** with the general grid, which we will finally update

Let us remember that by annulling these seven grades given by that student in question we are not totally erasing his evaluation work (her text-feedback is still visible to the peer who suffered it and he also continues to receive a grade as an evaluator). But we are doing it out of justice with the grade that the others receive, who now see the weakest member of the jury disappear from this panel.

We don't do this to 'lower' or 'raise' the grade of those colleagues you've checked. It just **stops influencing** his average grades. So, if this reviewer we're impeaching had given a low grade, now that grade will go up. And *viceversa*, if he had a high grade, now that grade will go down. In both cases we hope that he is approaching a more 'fair' grade (Definition always so controversial. Let's be satisfied with understanding it as: «***the one the teacher would have awarded in his place***»)

And in the section *Overrid Grade for Assessment*, it will be enough for us not to 'cancel' that calculated grade for her review –which was already low before and now, moreover, it will even drop a little more– or, if we prefer, we can manually put the one we decide.

Opposite case: students who despite having a brilliant grade for their submission received a very low grade evaluating others or we simply know personally their good record and suspect that they do not deserve such a bad result. Here it is very possible that **it is us to blame, for writing a confusing rubric** (we have failed to describe what we meant or we have not covered all the possible cases, so that the students were not able to assess coherently) or, worse, that we are facing specific situations of 'excess knowledge'.

In the case of 'excess knowledge' we are dealing with a student who applies correct criteria but not explained in the classroom **so we cannot demand it from the others**, leaving him alone, reviewing far from the majority, but obviously we do not wish to penalize neither him for his knowledge nor his classmates for not reaching that level.

If this is the case, we can also reduce their weightings so as not to punish those exercises assessed and then, in the section *Override grade for assessment*, manually give them the high mark they did deserve as reviewers.

Adjusting the review of the 'best' reviewers:

At the opposite pole of the ranking we find those students who have a high grade for their assessment. Notice what happens if we access their assessments and weight them up (from the original x1 to the maximum x16 we know). By overweighting them we will be modifying not their grade –since they probably already got a 100%, so they cannot go any higher– but **the grade of the exercises they reviewed**, which will now become fairer. In other words, the rest of the evaluators will no longer carry so much weight –those who evaluated worse, by giving a higher or lower grade than deserved– and that average will be closer to the criteria of these good evaluators. It is as if, instead of us evaluating fairly, we delegated that task to those who we trust are doing well. On the other hand, the rest of the jurors will now see their distance from the consensus somewhat more penalized, as the latter is now ratified by a smaller dispersion (the standard deviation of the whole decreases, as there are now 'sixteen' jurors supporting this new consensus). Perhaps with a *Very Lax* or *Lax* strategy it will be less noticeable, but if we were applying *Strict* or *Very strict* that penalty will be accentuated somewhat more.

In addition, another usefulness of reviewing what these good students have done is to look **at the exceptions.** Thus, if of their seven exercises evaluated, in six they get the maximum grade but there is a seventh one that seems to have given them problems, it is still convenient that we enter manually to see what is happening there in case it is a case of submission that does not fit well with our rubric or with a case of excess of knowledge as the ones commented before.

Adjusting the evaluation of the laziest:

This other pattern of behavior is visually very easy to detect. Here we look for a student who may have taken the job lightly and shown **a repetitive pattern of grades** (all tens, all zeros, all fives). At a glance will detect if we are facing any case like this. In all the courses I have met a student who perhaps did not have time to check his classmates as they should or thought he could go unnoticed by doing a quick pass through the rubric. In this case, all his reviews should be weighted as 'zero', to remove him from those juries in which he participated and, furthermore, manually grade him with the mark we consider he deserves.

And again, after pressing *Save*, remember to *Re-calculate* the grades.

Adjust evaluations from the opposite side, that of the reviewed students:

When we looked at the left column we had found mixed red and black blocks, in fact it is common to find the two colors mixed together. These are submissions which, although we had assigned them their seven evaluators, some of these jurors did not comply. And, now the opposite, it is not the fault of the author of the submission in question that the others did not comply, nor is it anyone's credit that many colleagues did evaluate them. So, in this column we will look at something else: whether there is a case in which someone has received so few evaluations that we are interested in **adding our own opinion**, entering into that task and evaluating it as one more jury, in order to increase the size of the sample.

To evaluate an exercise ourselves, we must **click on the title** of the task, which will give us access to its evaluation screen.

The menus remind us of the ones we have just seen for the *Assessment Settings*, in fact, they are the same in the upper area, but let's not get distracted: in this case we are no longer supervising the evaluation made by Belen but now **the submission of Saul**. Notice in the illustration on the right how two new buttons have appeared. Two buttons that we did not see while judging the reviewer: *Delete Submission* and Assess. Let's start with the latter.

By clicking on the title of
a submission we access its
evaluation screen

The Great Pyramid of Giza
Assessed submission

Attached, my response
by SAUL SEIJAS
modified on 30/05/2030...

*Well, in my opinion, the key to the
documentary we've seen in class
is in the fact that..*

Assesment
by BELEN BOVEDA
Grade 7 of 10

Assessment form ▸

▼ Assessment settings

Assessment weight   1 ⇕

Calculated grade for   2,7
assessment

Override grade for   Not overrid
assessment

Feedback for the reviewer    Paragrap

Up to this point, we had made decisions
that **affected the reviewer Belen**...

... Now we move on to
judge Saul's exercise

We can make it public to
the rest of the class

Respect the grade given by
your colleagues (that 6.8)
or grade it directly by us →

Give feedback to him →

The Great Pyramid of Giza
My submission

Attached, my response
by SAUL SEIJAS
modified on 30/05/2030...

*Well, in my opinion, the key to the
documentary we've seen in class
is in the fact that..*

Delete submission   Assess

Assesment
by EVA EGUREN
Grade 6 o 10

Assessment form ▸

Assesment
by RUBEN RAMOS
Grade 7 of 10

Assessment form ▸

Assesment
by ANA ALONSO
Grade 7 of 10

Assessment form ▸

Assesment
by BELEN BOVEDA
Grade 7 of 10

Assessment form ▸

▼ Feedback for the author

☐ Publish submission

Calculated grade for   6,8
submission

Override grade for   Not over
submission

Feedback for the author   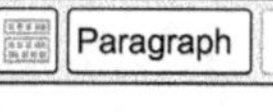 Paragraph

Not overriden
10
9
8
7

Assess By means of this **Assess** button we can enter to review the submission, as one more evaluator sitting beside the rest of the jurors, and fill in the rubric (in its entirety) so that we could impose our own criteria and the scores we consider it deserves –by weighing ourselves up, up to that maximum of x16–. Automatically, both the average grade **of the exercise** and the grade **received by the reviewers** will vary, as a new consensus will also be generated with our contribution to the panel. This tool is great when we see that a submission is receiving contradictory evaluations or we believe it is valuable to be able to provide a more correct review. However, before using it, please bear in mind the following limitation.

We already mentioned in the *Assessment* phase that, once saved, the review made by any participant **can be freely modified, but –be warned– it can no longer be deleted**. This is also true for teachers: if you enter *Re-Asses,* Moodle will ask you to fill all the fields before leaving the screen. The way to mitigate our numerical weight in that court would be to weigh ourselves 'x 0'. And the way to mitigate our moral weight, not to identify ourselves, since in the author's eyes we will continue to be an anonymous reviewer, like the rest of those who have participated in evaluating this exercise.

This has been frustrating for me when, as a teacher, I have considered that some of the questions evaluated demanded a clear answer, because they were objective –and that is what I wanted to show my students with my contribution–. But, at the same time, I did not want to impose my criteria on some other aspect of the rubric, which were more subjective or of free evaluation and in which I preferred not to lecture. Unfortunately, the weighting will refer to the whole rubric. It will not be possible to multiply x16 for one criterion and x0 for another at the same time.

Next, and totally different from *Assessing,* we find the menu to **grade the submission directly**. That is, using the lower menu to change from of *Not overriden* to any other grade selected from the drop-down menu. Here we will only rectify that grade received by the author –not that of the jury, whose consensus remains the same as before and whose internal penalties remain the same–. In the illustration on the next page you can see how I have rectified Belen's grade for the submission. Instead of the 3 that her classmates awarded her, I've manually put a 2. Moodle now shows me both: the current one and the rectified one. **You can always undo it**, just by re-activating *Not overriden*.

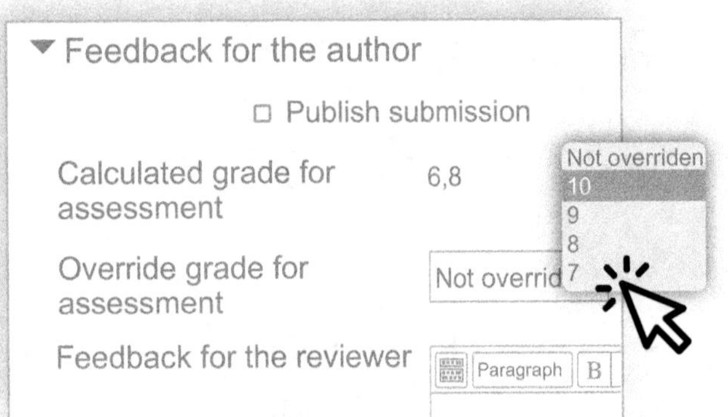

Also, the *Feedback* you write here is different. It is called For the Author and will be much more preponderant than the other one –*Overall*–, since as we will see later it will appear to the student in his main screen of the workshop, separated from the rest of the evaluators and, more important, this one will be shown signed by You.

Another difference between **Assessing** a submission in detail and limiting ourselves to **Grading** it numerically is that while we can do the former during both the *Assessment* and *Grading* phases, the latter can only be done over the second one.

Now that we know how to manually modify grades we will better decode **those two new symbols** used in the results grid to highlight these artificial changes made by the teacher:

> @ **The at**: indicates, next to a number, that the assessment of a certain participant has been weighted with a value different from 1. A 'zero' when its revision has been overlooked and between 2 and 16 when, on the contrary, we have multiplied its weight.

> – **The stud**: indicates that the teacher has manually invalidated a grade, which will now appear in red next to the new, valid, in green. It works the same whether the grades are for the assessment –small ones– or for the submission –which will appear as large ones as they modify an average–.

After making all the changes **remember to click on Recalculate grades** for the new results to take effect

The '@' indicates which reviewers are being weighted upwards (**as here to EVA x16**) or, conversely, downwards (like to **BELEN x0**), which is also changing the averages (that of Saul's exercise, formerly 6.8 now down to 6.1)

Although Belen's classmates awarded her a 3 on average, I have **manually lowered that score by one point**, hence Moodle now shows both

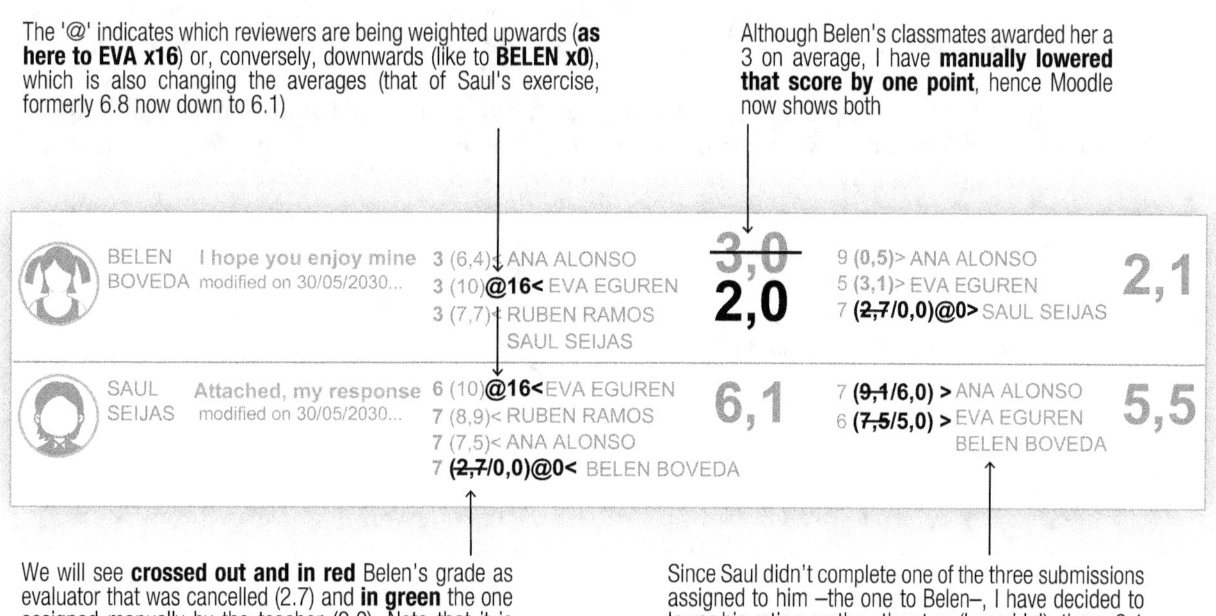

We will see **crossed out and in red** Belen's grade as evaluator that was cancelled (2.7) and **in green** the one assigned manually by the teacher (0.0). Note that it is reflected the same in its equivalent on the right column (Belen reviewing Saul) as here on the left (Saul receiving evaluation from Belen)

Since Saul didn't complete one of the three submissions assigned to him –the one to Belen–, I have decided to lower his rating on the other two ('override'), those 9.1 and 7.5 which previously gave him an average of 8.3. Now I have **manually given him a 6 and a 5**, that is, not for evaluating 'incorrectly', but incomplete

Delete submission

This *Delete Submission* button is the drastic method that Moodle makes available for those problematic cases with no other possible solution –which are more common than we would like–. For example, a student who has submitted an exercise by mistake or out of laziness that does not respond at all to what was requested. The fact is that when their fellow reviewers try to apply a rubric to it –by definition restricted and incapable of adapting to something like that– the assessments end up being so disparate and incoherent that **it would be unfair to penalise those jurors** for straying from any note of consensus, since it is not their fault that the measuring instrument did not provide for this situation.

Remember that although we could devalue the opinion of a jury so that it did not influence the rating, the other way round it was not possible to make the unfair result of a participation not influence it back. That's why in these cases the elimination of the exercise is the fairest method for everyone, but let's keep in mind that besides the fact that **this submission becomes unrecoverable** –automatically–, the grades of those who reviewed it will also be deleted, although the latter **will only be reflected in their averages the next time we click on *Re-calculate* grades**.

With the other methods we have seen so far, we could do endless tests, repent, change, recalculate and check the result. But there is no way back if you *Delete* a submission.

□ Publish submission

And on the contrary, if we consider an exercise «exemplary» or usable by others, the option *Publish submission* allows us to make it visible to the rest of the participants in the workshop when it is closed. This way, it will be accessible not only to the reviewers, but also **to the rest of the class, without exceptions**: whether they participated in the workshop or not, and regardless of the group mode we set up – separate, visible, etc. Everyone will be able to see this delivery **and the name of its author**. Moodle teachers are reminded of which submissions they have chosen to publish distinguishing them from the rest by a small **coloured background** in the control panel.

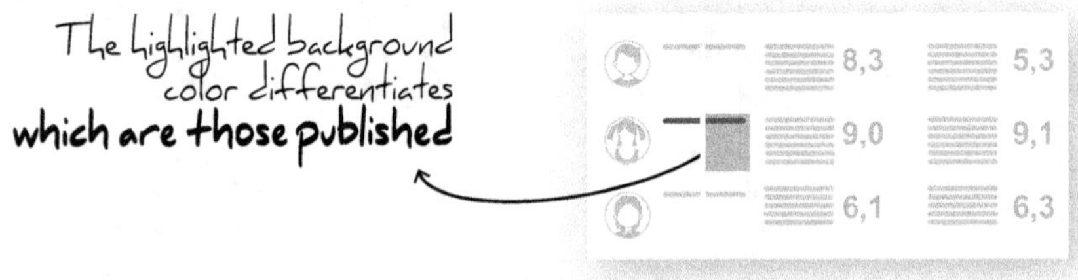

Finally, the Workshop Toolbox hides two reset buttons. One is practically harmless, the other, on the other hand, **extremely dangerous**.

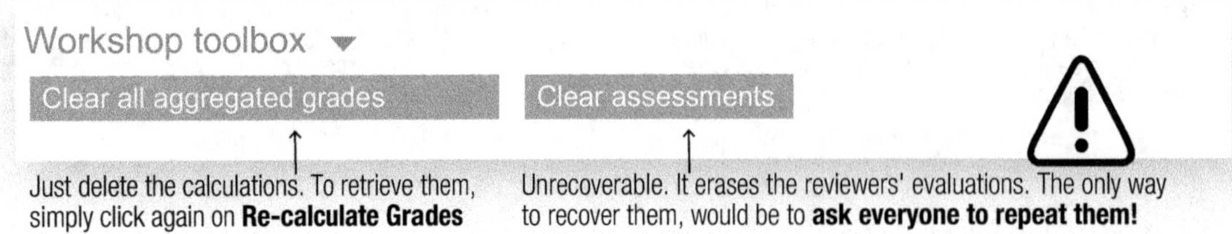

Closed

Teachers:
By simply 'closing' the workshop, **the grades are published** and added to the Gradebook, if it was configured

Students:
They will finally know both the grades and the feedbacks received by their peers and the teacher

Closing the workshop

The main consequence of closing the workshop is (woowoo!) that the students will finally know their grades –that is, what they were most interested in– and these will also **automatically turn to the *Gradebook*** if we had set it up that way. Until this moment, all the tests, corrections, recalculations and other data-cooking we did during the *Grading* phase remained private. As soon as we confirm that we *Close* the Workshop we uncover the surprise. And how does Moodle show them to the students? As teachers, it's not easy for us to find out what they're looking at at the moment –not even if we try to change role now, as we didn't participate in the previous phases either–. And it turns out that the screen they see is quite different from ours. Notice in the illustration how **Moodle indicates both ratings to them in clear boxes at the top of the screen**. But:

1. While by this point in the story teachers have become familiar with the terms *Grade for submission* and *Grade for assessment*, a student who finds them for the first time may be led to misunderstandings. In my first course I discovered to my horror –and already well advanced the four-month period– that among the students the following interpretation had been extended: that the first one was the grade that **the teacher was giving them** (!) and the second one was the one that colleagues had given each other when reviewing by pairs. That is to say, even when we had already held several workshops, they had not assimilated that they were the only ones grading each other and that, more importantly, making that evaluation conscientiously and ethically was the best way to continue obtaining points in the second phase. And this despite the fact that I had warned them about it both orally in the classroom and in writing in the course handbook. From that moment on, I started using the text field immediately above, the famous ***Conclusion*** of the workshop we know from *Adjustments*, to include a **clarifying tag** that would make the origin of each of these two digits very clear.

2. If a student has participated only in **one of the two tasks** –submitting their exercise or assessing others– Moodle will only show him **one box**, instead of leaving blank or using the other one to explicitly indicate the 'zero' that would correspond to that omission, which would certainly have been more clarifying.

Next they will see their own submission, then our *Feedback* to the student –if we had written it to this particular exercise– and then all those submissions that we would have decided to *publish*, including the name of their authors. Finally, the list of submissions that this student would have had to evaluate.

Now, didn't we miss something very important there? If you check again the sections you will be surprised by an **unjustifiable omission** in the final screen of this activity that we insist is so useful to «*learn twice*...» What is it?

What Saul sees **after the closing:**

The Great Pyramid of Giza

Closed ●

Conclusion ▼

Congratulations, 67 students have participated and with fantastic results. Below, your *Grade for submission* corresponds to...

← The instructions for submission or evaluation disappear and this place is now occupied by the 'Conclusion' of the teacher

← Convenient clarification

Your grades ▼

Grade for submission	Grade for assessment
6,1 / 10,0	**5,5 / 10,0**

← His two grades. And if he had only participated in one of the two phases, it would only indicate that one. (Instead of a more clear 'Zero' for the omissions)

Your submission ▼

Attached, my response by **SAUL SEIJAS**
Submitted on Wednesday, 15 April 2030, 17:55

 Feedbak by Dr. DANIEL GARCÍA

Great, Saul, I see that in your exercise you've applied...

← After submission, the 'Author Feedback', if written by the teacher

Published submissions ▼

My Essay on the Pyramids by **RUTH GARCIA**
Submitted on Thursday, 16 April 2030, 17:55

My answer by **BLANCA GONZÁLEZ**
Submitted on Thursday, 16 April 2030, 19.40

← Below, as Published Submissions, the same are shown to all participants, without filtering by group

Assigned submissions to assess ▼

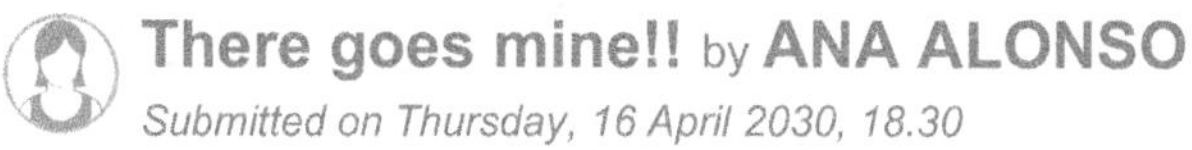
There goes mine!! by **ANA ALONSO**
Submitted on Thursday, 16 April 2030, 18.30

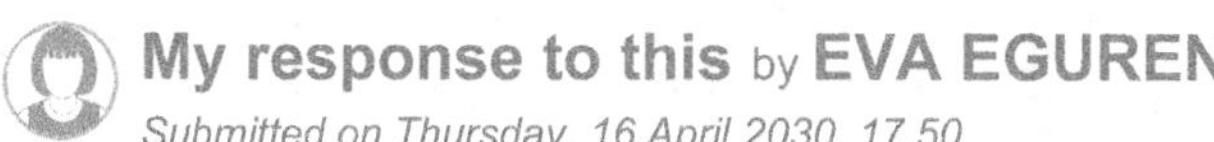
My response to this by **EVA EGUREN**
Submitted on Thursday, 16 April 2030, 17.50

← Finally, it allows him to see again the ones he had to asses himself

 Feedbak by Dr. DANIEL GARCÍA

In the case of your evaluation of Eva's answer I think you might have considered that...

← And the feedback as a reviewer, if we had written it

As it turns out, what the students are missing on that final screen is no more and no less than the **reviews and feedbacks received** (!). Surprisingly, they will have to go a step further to see them, **by clicking on the title of their own exercise**, which – if they don't know this circumstance – doesn't seem to be their priority at the moment.

I am afraid that all over the planet much of the great merit and the costly didactic fruits of all these processes of peer-assessment we teachers carry out with great effort are buried and wasted under that simple final step. Since I discovered it (remember that we teachers do not have access to that screen as the student sees it, so unless we ask someone to show it to us we will not be able to know it) I have extended the final list that I mentioned above and I advise to include the following mention as a punch line to the Conclusion

> *Congratulations on your participation. XX students have submitted their work, and XX of you have participated in reviewing others', of which [...] bla bla...*
>
> *The Grade* **for the submission** *refers to the exercise you submitted, while the Grade* **for the assessment** *refers to that second task of reviewing your colleagues'*
>
> *You can see the feedback that your colleagues have left for you* **by clicking on the title of your own exercise***.*

In these evaluations received, each rubric is broken down by section, as well as any feedback left by their colleagues. They take up a lot of space, which seems to be why Moodle has chosen not to display them on the main screen but to devote a separate one.

These evaluations received will be anonymous –provided we don't have the opposite set up in *Permissions*–. As we know, we can make sure this is the case by using the *Check permissions* tab, with the only exception of the 'self-assessment' of own exercises, which, if any, will appear first.

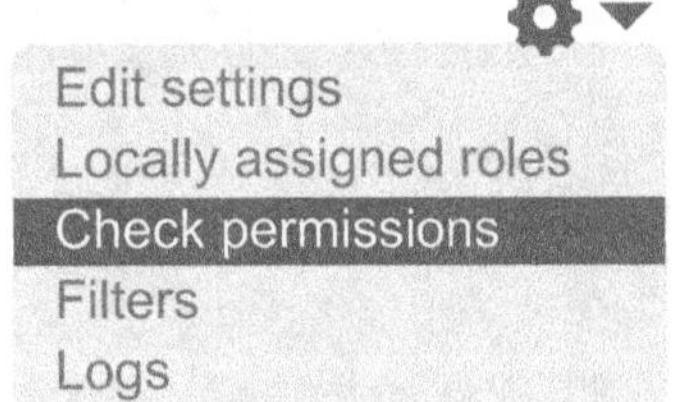

The teacher's will appear last, and not differenciated the others, so when You address the student through the *Global feedback*, **don't forget to identify yourself** if necessary, as Moodle will not do this for us.

The other piece of information shown is the *Weighting* of each assessment –when it is different from 'one'– as it is influencing the final grade received for the exercise.

The Great Pyramid of Giza

Closed ●

Conclusión ▼

Congratulations, 67 students have participated
results. Below, your *Grade for submission* corres

Sus calificaciones ▼

Grade for submission	Grade assess
6,1 / 10,0	5,5 /

Your submissi

Attached, my response by S
Submitted on Wednesday, 15 April 2030, 17:5

 Feedbak by Dr. DANIEL GARC

Great, Saul, I see that in your exercise you've

Published submissions ▼

My Essay on the Pyramids b
Submitted on Thursday, 16 April 2030, 17:55

My answer by BLANCA GONZ
Submitted on Thursday, 16 April 2030, 19.40

Assigned submissions to assess ▼

There goes mine!! by ANA AL
Submitted on Thursday, 16 April 2030, 18.30

My response to this by EVA E
Enviado el 6 de noviembre de 2030, 17:50

 Feedbak by Dr. DANIEL GARC

In the case of your evaluation of Eva's answe

The Great Pyramid of Giza
My submission

Instructions for submission ▶

Attached, my response
by SAUL SEIJAS
Submitted on Wednesday, 15 April 2030, 17:55

Well, in my opinion, the key to the documentary
we've seen in class is in the fact that..

Assessment
Grade: 6 of 10

Assessment form ▼

Criterion 1
Did he answer the question?
- ○ No. It's gone off the rails
- ◉ Yes, although not in depth
- ○ Yes, satisfactorily

Did he respect the requested length?
- ○ No
- ◉ Yes

Overall feedback ▶

Assessment
Grade: 7 of 10

Assessment form ▶
Overall feedback ▶

Assesment
Grade: 7 of10
Weight: 16

Assessment form ▶
Overall feedback ▶

Is it reversible? What can I change after closing the workshop

The closure of the workshop is a leap that we can always undo. Now, it's quite possible that your students have already had access to their grades —because by the time one discovers it and spreads the word via WhatsApp in a matter of minutes everyone will know theirs–. Therefore, my reservations before moving on to *Closed* derive more from this public aspect, since technically it is possible to go back to any other phase of the workshop that we want to rectify something, but, as we intuitively know, any subsequent modification of a grade **could imply having to recalculate, as a knock on effect, those of many other participants** and thus force us to offer some public explanations.

Having said that, let's see what the platform technically allows us to update, rectify or eliminate, from the most obvious and simple to the least expected:

AFTER CLOSING THE WORKSHOP: POSSIBLE CHANGES **WITHOUT INFLUENCE ON GRADES:**

1. **The teacher's *Conclusion*.** Logically, we can continue to update it at any time, without hindrance, since it was filled in in the main *Settings*. Any retouching we make to it will automatically become visible to those entering the workshop.

2. *Feedback for the reviewers*, again, unimpeded. You will discover that you can enter by clicking on each assessment and modify those text fields that were later reflected on their main screen. Even the *Weighting*, if modified, would be published, but it would still not influence the grades as long as you do not click on *Re-calculate grades*. And that button disappeared, of course, since we closed the workshop.

3. On the contrary, the two types of feedback-comments for authors, both the ***Global*** and the ***Feedback for the author***, simply require going back to the previous phase in order to be edited. We could go back, to the *Grading phase*, a few minutes to rectify them and they would be updated as soon as we closed the workshop again.

4. Editorial little adjustments **in the criteria of the *Rubric*** and its details. You can also enter and modify those statements, although, of course, this is delicate. It might not be honest to change its essence now, in hindsight, when the students have already filled in that form according to its literalness. Let's think about spelling or mere stylistic retouching, otherwise we could cause misunderstandings. In fact, if we remove some of the criteria —or their intermediate levels, for example 'Regular'– they will automatically disappear from the participants, even if they had chosen it. So they will start to see on screen some review forms with some differences from the ones they filled in. But this will not change their grades for the exercise.

CHANGES THAT **DO INFLUENCE** THE GRADES AFTER THE WORKSHOP IS CLOSED:

5. The **grades that we entered manually** –with that *Override grade* option– will continue to tread on the original ones, being saved in memory and shown to us with that double format on screen, but none will have any effect –not even if we reopen and close the workshop again– until we *Re-calculate* the grades by pressing that button. Then yes.

6. **Re-assess** an exercise is also perfectly possible whenever you go back to the *Assessment* phase. You can then decide whether or not to *re-calculate* the grades so they take effect when closed.

7. Changes in the weights of individual reviewers are always public. If with the workshop closed I decide to give Belen a higher weight in any of the juries in which she participated, it will be public both to her and to the authors of those other exercises. However, this is only for information purposes, since, again, in order to have an effect on the grades we will need to *Re-calculate*.

8. We could also enter the *Rubric* to edit not only the wording of its criteria, but also its numerical values, or even delete an intermediate one. Here Moodle is restrictive: the grades continue to be saved as they were given at the time when each reviewer was evaluated. The grades for the submission, therefore, do not change. Even if we click on *Re-calculate* again. However, the grades for the assessment do undergo adjustments and are recalculated. If we close the workshop again, they will become public.

> Making changes to the numerical values of the rubric can make **a lot of sense when thinking about future reuses**. If you regret one and want to save the changes to use the same workshop next year, it is very useful to do so. However, if you change the wording, **the participants in the current one will see your new version**. So, for any kind of change it is more advisable to **duplicate** the current workshop, hide the copy, and work on it.

9. The total grade for the exercise, as assigned in the main *Settings* –both for the submission and the assessment– can always be changed further, and Moodle will automatically adjust the grades –and include them in the *Gradebook*– without any further action. This could also be edited at any of the above stages.

10. What about changing the ***Grading Strategy*** (from *Rubric* to *Comments*, for example) and reopening the workshop? As we saw, technically it is perfectly possible. All evaluations and ratings are saved and would only be changed where the participants themselves re-enter and evaluate. The others are kept in their notes. In fact, reversing this change again (now go back from *Comments* to *Rubric*) would retrieve all that original information. [But remember that pernicious effect explained on page 43].

Reusing the workshop

After finishing the workshop it is possible to make all that time investment profitable by reusing it as many times as we need. We can generate a copy of the activity, as with any other, by clicking on ***Duplicate***:

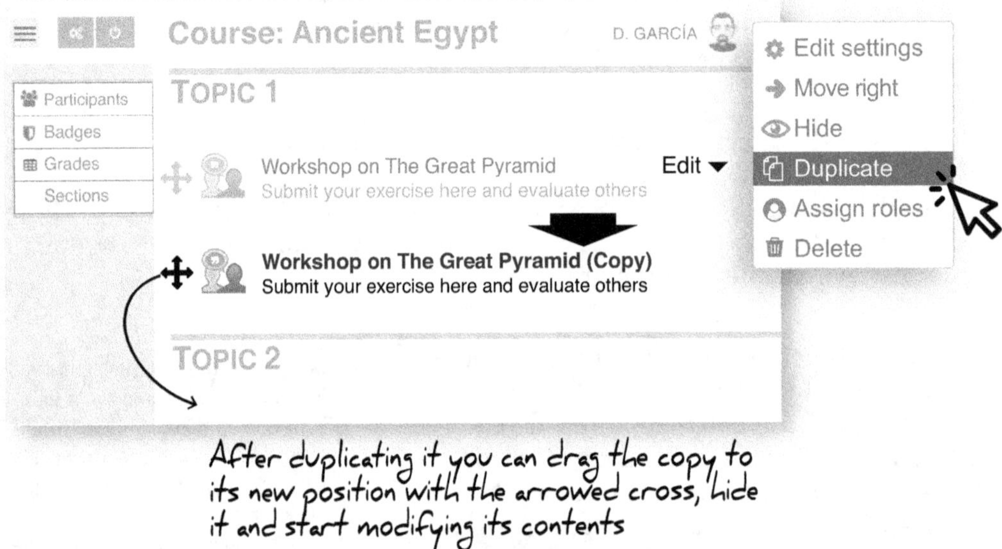

After duplicating it you can drag the copy to its new position with the arrowed cross, hide it and start modifying its contents

The new version, which the system baptizes with the surname '***copy***', will appear without any trace of having been used by the students, that is, empty of answers to the exercise, without allocation or, of course, reviews or grades. All user information disappears and the module is ready to be reused.

However, your possible time settings –such as past **dates and times of openings and/or closings**– will also be copied, so if they were enabled in the original we will now have to update them.

Please note that the copy **will appear at the same phase** as the original workshop when it is duplicated, so it is advisable to hide it temporarily –***Hide*** menu–, so as not to confuse those students who might find it on the cover of the course by suddenly inviting them to hand it in or to co-evaluate. We will return the workshop to the first phase –*Settings*– to spruce it up, modify and edit its parts before making it visible again as if it were a totally new activity.

The Sisyphus rock will now have climbed halfway up by itself.

NOTES